I DIDN'T SEE THAT COMING

ANDREA BEGLEY

BBC
BOOKS

Andrea Begley won *The Voice UK* in 2013, and her first album, *The Message*, was released by Capitol Records later the same year. When Andrea was six years old, she started losing her sight, and now only has 10% residual vision, but she's never let that stop her. When she applied for *The Voice UK*, she was working as a civil servant, studying for a Masters Degree in law, learning the guitar and gigging around Belfast. Andrea lives in County Tyrone.

1 3 5 7 9 10 8 6 4 2

Published in 2013 by BBC Books, an imprint of Ebury Publishing.
A Random House Group Company.

The Voice UK is produced by Wall to Wall Media, part of the Shed Media Group, in co-production with Talpa. Global hit, *The Voice*, is created and owned by Dutch media entrepeneur John De Mol's company Talpa, and is currently produced in over 50 countries worldwide.

Andrea Begley management – Twenty First Artists

Text © Andrea Begley 2013
Andrea Begley has asserted her right to be identified as the author of this Work in accordance with the Copyright, Designs and Patents Act 1988.
Plate sections: all images from *The Voice UK* © Wall to Wall Media Limited 2013; Andrea with Lulu © Edward Lloyd; all other photographs © Andrea Begley

The Random House Group Limited Reg. No. 954009

Addresses for companies within the Random House Group can be found at
www.randomhouse.co.uk

A CIP catalogue record for this book is available from the British Library.

ISBN: 978 1 849 90487 2

The Random House Group Limited supports the Forest Stewardship Council® (FSC®), the leading international forest-certification organisation. Our books carrying the FSC label are printed on FSC®-certified paper. FSC is the only forest-certification scheme supported by the leading environmental organisations, including Greenpeace. Our paper procurement policy can be found at www.randomhouse.co.uk/environment

Commissioning editor: Lorna Russell
Project editor: Lizzy Gaisford
Copyeditor: Lindsay Davies
Proofreader: Wendy Hollas
Production: Alex Goddard

Typeset by seagulls.net
Printed and bound by CPI Group (UK) Ltd, Croydon CR0 4YY

To buy books by your favourite authors and register for offers visit
www.randomhouse.co.uk

My book is dedicated to all those who have moulded me emotionally, academically or indeed musically over the years to become the person that I am today. You all know who you are, and you all know how much I appreciate your love and faith in me.

FOREWORD

I am standing in a back room of a TV studio chatting to Danny O'Donoghue, lead singer of The Script, one of my favourite bands in the world. Somewhere in the background I can hear Will.i.am from The Black Eyed Peas talking to my mum. I later find out that at that very moment, she is actually trending on Twitter. A short while later, my Aunt Philomena will sing a duet with Sir Tom Jones. So, just a normal Begley family night out then! How on earth did this happen?

Winning *The Voice* that night was one of the most surreal moments of my life. Since that day, I've gone on to do things I would never have thought possible, and to be frank, one of those is writing this book. When I was first asked about penning a book, I have to admit I was a little uncertain of what to think. I understood that winning the show meant people were interested in 'my story', for want of a better phrase, but at the same time I have always felt that winning *The Voice* was merely a starting point, a first step on what I hope will be a very long and successful career.

Not in a bazillion years did I think I'd be singing at sports stadiums, recording albums or writing a book when I entered *The Voice* in the summer of 2012. So, what I have tried to do in these pages is just give you a flavour of the path that took me to that crazy night a year later when the British public voted me as their winner. I haven't spoken about every single minute detail of my life up until that point, because I don't feel that now is the time to do that. Instead I have just tried to give you a picture of some of the most pivotal moments along the way: obviously my visual impairment, but also my own long-standing involvement with music before the show as well as, of course, my time on *The Voice*. Being so closely involved with Danny and the other three coaches as well as all the other amazing people I met on that programme is the focus of this book and I hope that by giving you a behind-the-scenes tour you will come to appreciate that brilliant show even more.

I have always enjoyed writing, whether it is creative writing, keeping a few diaries or, most pertinently, songwriting. So this book is really just an extension of that passion – a few stories and thoughts to give you a snapshot of some important moments in my life, what I've done and where I have come from. Hopefully these anecdotes will tell you how I have reached this point where I am recording my debut album and have the most exciting times ahead of me.

I am only twenty-six so I would like to think that I have a lot of living left to do yet, not just in terms of music but life in general. Hopefully beyond this point there is still plenty of room for growth, development and further achievement. For me, then, my aim was that this book would be an insightful, interesting and, above all, fun snapshot of my life now and how I got here – a metaphorical and literal opening chapter.

CHAPTER 1

EARLY CHALLENGES

It is quite difficult for me to remember exactly when I first started to notice problems with my eyes, because I was fairly young when the initial symptoms started appearing. The condition that has impaired my vision is called glaucoma, but actually that in itself came from a pretty unusual problem called juvenile rheumatoid arthritis. When I was three and a half years old, I developed a limp in one of my ankles – like lots of kids do from time to time – and initially my parents thought that I had sprained it or fallen awkwardly, or maybe even broken it somehow. However, the limp didn't improve or go away and so Mum took me to various doctors until a proper diagnosis was made, which was when we first learned that I had juvenile rheumatoid arthritis. Rheumatoid arthritis is quite unusual in youngsters, and it is obviously something generally associated with older people. However, as my family discovered, it can also affect children.

In essence, rheumatoid arthritis is an auto-immune condition where your body attacks itself because it thinks there is something wrong with the joints, but there is actually nothing wrong at all; however, that's how the body sees it and this causes various problems. One of these problems is difficulties with your eyesight. In my case, what initially started with my ankle eventually led to me developing cataracts in my eyes and, ultimately, glaucoma. So the condition evolved in quite a complicated way, but essentially the specific cause of my visual impairment was the subsequent glaucoma. This has caused the majority of my sight loss since the age of about six.

My earliest memories of the condition beginning to take hold are quite vague – my sight didn't stop overnight but instead suffered a gradual decline – and I can remember quite a few things about being completely sighted. I can remember watching films, going to places on holidays and seeing people very clearly, so in fact when people describe things to me now I can often imagine what they are talking about in great detail, because I still have a lot of memories of seeing things as a fully sighted person. For example, I do remember what colours look like and there are a number of films that I can sit back and watch that I saw years previously and still recall exactly what happens, because I have that visual memory from seeing it the first time. So in many ways I grew up with a fair amount of vision. Consequently, while I can't see things clearly now, I still approach life as a sighted person because that is the way I grew up as a young girl.

I was always missing quite a bit of school because I was in and out of hospital like a yo-yo, undergoing operation after operation on my eyes (I think I notched up about twenty-three by adulthood). The removal of the cataracts was obviously a big deal and then after that it was predominantly glaucoma control. The main problem with the disease is that it causes high pressure in your eyes which consequently ends up damaging your optic nerve – unfortunately your optic nerve cannot be replaced or transplanted. So my operations would invariably involve the insertion of tubes to try and ease the pressure in my eyes that was being caused by the glaucoma. Doctors tried really hard both here and in Glasgow and London to try and stave off the high pressure, but my disease was just very hard to control; some people can control it reasonably well with nothing more than eyedrops, but my glaucoma just fluctuated so much it was difficult to get a handle on. It didn't really start to calm down until I hit my late teens and early twenties. Ultimately, however, in the years leading up to that calmer period, my optic nerve had been irreparably damaged and this led to my sight loss.

Back as an eight-year-old, I'd started flying to eye hospitals, or hospitals with specialist eye units, in Glasgow and London as well as visiting those in Northern Ireland that could help me. I don't really have all that many memories of those trips. I can vaguely remember going to the Windsor Eye Unit near London, I also went to places like the Royal Eye Infirmary in Glasgow.

Funnily enough, it wasn't so much the operations and the tubes that bothered me at that age, it was the anaesthetic. I knew that what they were doing to my eyes was to try to help me, but what terrified me most was being knocked out beforehand. I never liked that sensation: to me as a young girl it was horrifying and I always used to get freaked out by that, because in my young mind it always felt like being unconscious was a kind of death.

I do have plenty of good memories of those early years too, though. A lot of the time I had to go to adult wards because, as I mentioned, my condition was very unusual for a child, so maybe there weren't necessarily the right specialists available in the children's wards. I do remember playing with other children in the various hospitals and also the nurses trying to make us all feel a bit more normalised. There would be toys to play with and other simple stuff like colouring-in pictures. I think I had every colouring-in book going, despite the fact that I couldn't really see the pictures sometimes. So there were some good memories but obviously I just wanted to get home, go back to school and do the stuff that everyone else my age was doing.

Unfortunately, the deterioration in my eyes continued despite the best efforts of the doctors and so from about the age of eight onwards I suffered the majority of my sight loss. However, as I had started my primary school as a sighted person, even when the deterioration progressed more noticeably I wanted to continue at the same place with my friends and teachers. School was literally just at the end of my road in my hometown of Pomeroy, in County Tyrone, Northern Ireland. It was great but obviously it wasn't set up to work with a visually impaired child. However, the attitude of my doctors was that if I could continue in a mainstream school with some adaptations, it would be more beneficial for me from an educational point of view than going to a specialist school for the blind. There was such a school in Northern Ireland but it was a good ninety minutes' round trip each day from where I lived, so for me that wasn't really a viable option. I wanted to stay at my school anyway so that was great news. However, being in a mainstream school meant that I didn't learn things like Braille. For the most part, in the early days especially, I would have managed with large print and someone like a classroom assistant who would have helped me with taking notes from the blackboard (or the white board as it then became!). So it really was just a case of managing as best we could in the circumstances.

My schools – both primary and secondary – really did try their best but I can't deny that a lot of the time things were difficult. The education system simply wasn't geared up for a blind or visually impaired child. Books weren't available in alternative formats, and I remember having to go round with massive piles of A3 enlargements, to the point where my school bag was enormous, crammed with all these oversized bits of paper. It weighed a ton. But that was the best way round it in the early days while I still had some limited vision; I could manage with large print to some degree.

However, as I headed into my teens and started secondary school, my vision continued to get worse. By the time I was studying for my GCSEs, my vision had deteriorated significantly, to the point where large print wasn't really much of a help to me any more. I would say I lost quite a lot of vision in my teens; up until the age of about fourteen, fifteen, I could still manage to get around a bit on my own but beyond that point I started to need people to guide me.

I inevitably had to start to learn to use a white cane and I really hated that. I suppose for me at that point there was a real stigma associated with it so I was very self-conscious. Plus I could still see just about enough to notice people looking at me using it. Consequently, for a long time I shied away from using the cane; it has really only been in the past maybe five or six years that I have thought, *Hold on a second, I need this to get around!* Now that I am older and more comfortable with my visual impairment, I actually don't give a stuff what people think, whether they look at me or not. It was probably just a case of getting used to the thing, because all teenagers have a hard time trying to grow into who they are as a person anyway, so to have that extra hurdle to overcome was something that I did feel very self-conscious about at the time.

In the meantime, I often wouldn't let people know just how poor my vision was. A major part of the confusion is caused by the fact that I wear glasses. People often think that because I wear glasses it means that I can see them, but it doesn't. I suppose the best way to explain it is that while I don't have a lot of vision, the tiny amount of useful vision that I do have is slightly enhanced by wearing glasses. When I was six the lenses were removed from my eyes, so I had to wear contacts, but to be honest they were not a huge amount of use to me because I had to wear lenses that were quite hard, rather than the soft ones people normally use. They were quite uncomfortable so it was just easier for me to wear glasses. My glasses merely enhance the blur and make the best of what I have got; it is not a huge amount of difference but it does help slightly so my optician has always advised me to continue to wear them for that reason.

I felt less awkward wearing glasses and, to be honest, I would sometimes not tell people I was visually impaired unless I really had to. Clearly sometimes it was completely obvious, but otherwise I just wouldn't mention it. They wouldn't necessarily know to look at me that I was stereotypically what someone might determine as 'blind'. I'm not entirely sure what 'blind' is supposed to look like anyway.

As an adult, I have had some involvement with the Royal National Institute for the Blind (RNIB) and so I have learned some really interesting statistics about visual impairment. One of the facts that always sticks with me is that something like only 2 per cent of people who are blind see absolutely nothing; the other 98 per cent of people have a spectrum of vision, right from people who have fairly clear vision, through to those who are partially sighted (some of my friends are partially sighted and would still be fit to read fairly normal size print) and onwards to people who are completely blind and see nothing, not even light and dark.

I am on that spectrum, so I am able to be registered blind. You know those charts at the opticians that you have to read, with rows of letters that get progressively smaller? They are called Snellen Charts and they measure your level of vision acuity. Once you reach a point on those charts where your vision is measured as being limited to a certain level, you are then able to be registered blind. I have been registered blind from the age of nine. Therefore my vision has been quite limited since then.

But that doesn't mean that I haven't been fit to see anything, it just means that my ability to do so has got less and less pronounced over the years. To the point now where all I really see are outlines, blurs, some colours – things like that. It is all very mushy. I can't really see things very distinctly; I can make out silhouettes or outlines, like the odd chair, but I would need to be very close to it. I can sometimes see colours but I wouldn't be able to recognise them all the time, it just depends.

At school, therefore, things were obviously more complicated for me because of my visual impairment. However, I am proud to say that I was always very good at school, in the sense that I really applied myself. Maybe it was just sheer stubbornness on my part, but I never wanted to be behind everybody else. I always felt that if I pushed myself enough I could probably achieve reasonably well when it came to my education. Actually, as it turned out, I did more than a lot of people, but I will come on to that later.

One question a lot of people ask me is how did I get my information at school? As I have said, I never learned Braille because I was in a mainstream school. At first, while I had some vision I had those enlarged A3 print-outs, plus I used large-print books and at home my parents and my sister Hannah (who is three years younger than me) would be brilliantly helpful by reading to me in the evenings, to try and keep me up-to-date with what was happening and to get through my textbooks as quickly as possible. Beyond that point though, as my vision got worse, I started to use a laptop, and enlarge the print on screen as big as I needed to.

After a while, however, as my eyesight worsened still further, even the laptop became useless to me as well, so I had to adapt and learn to use speech software. This was just as I started my A levels and, I have to tell you, the software was a revelation! Fantastic. It completely transformed what I could do, and it felt so incredibly liberating. The best way I can describe it is it's like using all the functions on the computer but without using a mouse, so it is all done by keyboard and via shortcut keystrokes. Although I am now totally used to the programme, it is actually quite complicated to use and initially I found it very difficult to get into, simply because I had been so used to looking and trying to squint at things for the most part. But I persevered and slowly started to get the hang of it and, once I realised how to use it and what it could do to help me, it made an extraordinary difference to my life.

Mind you, I have to be honest and say that because the voice is electronic – it sounds a bit like Stephen Hawking – for the first few days after I got the speech software my main source of entertainment was to type curse words and stupid sentences into it, just because I thought this was absolutely hilarious. After a while, of course, the novelty wore off and I actually knuckled down to using it as the constructive tool it was meant to be!

The software will tell me what I have typed and read things back to me. It means I can use emails and the Internet and all that there, which is great. Once I got used to how it worked, it meant that I could do things on the same basis as everyone else. There are certain things that the software struggles with, such as pictures and graphics, for example, so you're always doing things on a largely textual basis, but I didn't mind that because it was still opening up masses of information to me in comparison to what I had been fit to access before.

I would never sit and complain, though; that's not me. I just like to crack on and succeed and take up the challenge! As a teenager, while I was determined to learn as much as the next person, I was also having to adapt to a condition that limited me not just in terms of education, but also with making friends and socialising. As a teenager you feel a bit awkward about yourself anyway, so to be learning to deal with my visual impairment as well did, at times, make life tricky.

I often found solace in both books and music, because those were things that I could do – not absolutely independently, perhaps, but for the most part on my own. That was crucial to me. Audio books I loved. We used to have a library session every week in school and for the first couple of years I would have used large-print books. Then it got to the point where I just could not see well enough and I was seriously struggling to use them, so the librarian suggested I get some audio books. Initially I wasn't that keen, to be honest, because as a kid I loved the *process* of reading. I didn't really like the idea of listening to the words rather than actually looking at the text on the page. I used to enjoy reading the words and seeing how they were spelt, consuming the text on the physical page. I feel lucky that for the first ten years I was fit to do that, to look at the actual text, which meant that I managed to build up a bit of a vocabulary and a decent knowledge of spelling (I was always quite a good speller). But beyond that age it started to become too difficult.

Coming from such a love of physical books, at first I wasn't particularly attracted to audio books. I just thought audio books were a different experience – they seemed less intimate, somehow. However, I gave them a try and in a very short space of time I loved them! Yes, it is a different kind of reading experience compared to looking at a page; it is a different way of taking in information. However, I just loved the fact it allowed me to get through books so quickly. By the age of around eleven, audio books really were my best option, and after that initial reluctance I absolutely loved them because I could just fly through the stories. I used to read books such as *Under the Hawthorn Tree*, or *To Kill a Mockingbird* and, like so many other children, I just adored all the Roald Dahl stories. So audio books became a great joy.

I can't stress enough also how much my family helped me too. My parents were amazing, so supportive. They were very proud of me for a lot of things that I achieved. And my sister Hannah was, too. She used to sit and read books for hours with me. Looking back I think it was pure cruelty on my part sometimes! She had to sit there endlessly reading all about Nazi Germany or all this stuff that she found really boring because she was three years younger than me. I used to say to her, 'I am doing you a favour: by the time you start to study all this stuff you will already know everything!' She was brilliant, though, so patient.

So you can see that as I grew through secondary school, there were things that were a challenge for me. But I never let that bother me. I was grand. I think there was a certain stubbornness on my part that made me just go for it all the more, because I always saw myself as the same as everyone else, and I wasn't going to allow myself to have dispensations beyond reason. I would have got some extra time in my exams but that was simply because it took me that bit longer to read things or to type things up or navigate my way through science diagrams – which were always a flaming nightmare! The fact I took a little longer was irrelevant to me – the main thing was that I could still do it.

Exams were there to be passed and I wanted the best grades possible. I set goals to achieve and I used to love it when I passed an exam and sometimes maybe got a certificate and that box had been ticked! Especially maths: I never wanted to look at maths again apart from when I was paying for something in a shop. Ha ha!

But no, I never expected or asked for special allowances or anything beyond what was a minimal necessity for me. That was very important because I didn't want to be seen as needing a whole lot of extra help or extra assistance. I wanted to achieve everything off my own bat, if you know what I mean.

When it came to my GCSE results, I got six A*s, three As and a B. The B was in maths and that really bugged me, I kept looking at the B and thinking, *Flippin' heck!* I wanted all As or A*s. When I read the results letter, I do remember thinking, *That is pretty good*, but I have always been a perfectionist and at times I am my own worst critic. I always just wanted to strive for the next level. I suppose, looking back as an adult on what it had taken for me to get to those GCSE results, it was an amazing achievement really, to be fair.

At that age, the next step was my three A levels, which I took in politics, history and religious education. I really enjoyed studying those subjects and although my sight was very poor by then, it was never going to stop me succeeding. In fact, I got three As and my score for politics was the third highest in the whole of Northern Ireland. I just really enjoyed studying that topic and I loved the classes, so the visual impairment was pretty irrelevant to me. I suppose now when you look back that is a big achievement too.

I feel very lucky about my education for several reasons. I was fortunate that I went to good schools and had good teachers. I know some visually impaired kids – and indeed lots of children in general – don't have people to push them, like their family or school, so I was very lucky there. Quite a lot of other visually impaired people I know have had to go and do further qualifications once they've left school just to try and bring themselves to the kind of level they need to make themselves employable.

From my own point of view, I never felt hard done by in terms of having to work harder or longer to get the grades. In fact, getting the trophies and certificates made it all the more worthwhile in the end – it felt especially sweet knowing how much harder I had had to work to attain that level of achievement. As I said, I felt lucky.

CHAPTER 2

NOTES AND MEDALS

As much as books and reading were a vital part of my life growing up, so too was music. All the way through my childhood, music was very much interwoven with my school and home. It was always a massive part of family life. At family parties and birthdays, everybody would get up and do their poem or their song – you always had to do your party piece! Same for weddings and any family gatherings: all the aunts, uncles and cousins would sing and play instruments. People would always be up dancing, there was just so much music around.

There were more than just family performances, too. My aunt, Philomena Begley, is a very well-known and highly respected country singer in Ireland. She was and still is a prominent figure in the country music scene here and beyond. She will regularly do gigs in England and Scotland and she has been to Nashville many times. Amazingly, in 2012 she celebrated fifty years in the music business. Fifty years! I've always said if I could hold out for anywhere near as long as that I would be very happy. What an incredible achievement.

With all this around me, it's perhaps not at all surprising that from a very young age I loved music. I absolutely adored all the singing and dancing, and I would join in enthusiastically at all these parties. We have lots of family videos from those years, from when I was as young as three, and I'm always singing away – nursery rhymes, pop tunes, Irish traditional songs, sometimes with a microphone, sometimes not, twirling about, giving it my all. As I got a little older, music continued to be something that I really enjoyed, and it became my favourite pastime.

From about the age of seven I played piano, and after a number of years I eventually got to Grade Six. I was still fit to read music in the early days although it would have been enlarged print but at least at first I was able to sit down with a piano teacher and read through my music books. So I did all my exams up to Grade Six but beyond that point I just didn't have the time to devote myself as much as was required to reach Grade Seven and Eight, not least because as my eyesight deteriorated my school work was obviously taking longer and longer. I played a bit of tin whistle as well but piano was my main instrument.

Music was always something that I was conscious of wanting to do as a pleasurable hobby outside of school, so I never really contemplated doing it for GCSE or A level, because I thought that that would make it too formal, too rigid. To me, it was always a joy to sit down at the piano and play, rather than having someone tell me I needed to practise three million times a day.

One thing I also did from a very young age was sing. When my dad later spoke to *The Voice* he said, 'She has never done singing, she has us tortured!', but obviously he was joking! I was always singing around the house. I suppose where other people would have turned to the TV or read a book, when my vision was getting worse singing was something that I took to like a duck to water. I just loved it. There was a kind of freedom there, in the sense that I didn't have to ask anyone to help me do it: I could just switch on a CD or my iPod and sing along. It was something that I could do completely independently.

It was this freedom that made me fall more and more in love with music. Clearly, for me, sport was very much off-limits – it was just not possible. I did it when I was much younger because I was still fit to see back then, but it kind of loses its appeal when you are always afraid of being knocked over or tripping or whatever. As a young kid I played outdoors and did all the stuff kids do, but with my eyesight deteriorating from the very early years of primary school, that didn't last long. Contact sport was totally off-limits and gradually, as my eyesight went, so too did pretty much every other physical-based pastime. So singing became even more important to me.

In Ireland they have these singing competitions called Feis, where local children take part in competitions from a very young age, even while they're still at primary school. I would always go to those to do a poem or to sing. You had to stand up on stage in front of the other children and an adjudicator, who would make notes and mark your performance. At first I didn't win or even come in the top three or so, but I didn't mind all that much, I just really loved taking part. A lot of the time I would come away without anything, which was obviously disappointing when they read out the names of the first, second and third places and unfortunately, once again, you weren't on the list. However, I do remember the reward afterwards was that there was a little tuck shop on the way home and we would always get crisps and a drink there. For young kids that always soothed the disappointment! I think it was towards the end of my primary school years before I actually won my first singing medal at one of these Feis.

I suppose now, when you look back at it, even at that very early stage these competitions were probably helping me in a way. Even though they were on such a small scale, they nonetheless involved me practising singing in front of people, planting that seed of learning how to perform and getting me used to an audience as well as being judged and critiqued. When you enter a TV show like *The Voice*, it is an inevitability that you are going to be critiqued by the coach, but also beyond that by the public too, so I think these early competitions were really good for me, because they got me used to that process very early on.

As I got older, the competitions I participated in had a broader reach, so it wasn't just local schools – there would be talent contests open to all-comers of a certain age. I had also been doing various competitions run by the GAA, the Gaelic Athletic Association. They have their own brilliant talent competition called Scór, based more in traditional Irish music which I've always loved. That style of music is very popular in Ireland and America in particular, and it has quite a distinct sound. Once again these performances would be in front of judges and often I would be coming away with a result that wasn't positive. On a number of occasions, though, I did come out on top and that was quite an achievement; you didn't win money, although you did receive a medal or trophy, but the most important thing was the pride and prestige of winning.

One really enjoyable part of all these competitions was that I never thought for a second that I was there taking part as a visually impaired person. To me I was competing as a singer on the same basis as everyone else. What the adjudicators said to me afterwards was predominantly about my singing and less so about my performance, and it was certainly nothing to do with my ability or inability to see. They were usually more focused on the vocals rather than stage presence, although the latter was sometimes commented on. 'Needs to engage more with the audience,' blah, blah, blah. I think sometimes they weren't necessarily aware that I couldn't see or how limited my vision was because, as usual, I would be wearing glasses.

However, I would never dismiss what they were saying because I knew I needed to improve my performance; that was something of which I was well aware. The problem is, the performance element has always been pretty difficult for me to tap into because I don't have the visual cues that everyone else does. Let me explain that a little bit more. For example, a lot of people don't realise but the way they perform on stage is essentially mimicry. They watch other performers either at concerts or perhaps on TV and subconsciously they mimic the body language they see, how they move and so on. But if you don't have that visual feedback, you can't do that. I knew improving my performance was required, and my parents and sister tried to give me tips at home, which is all well and good, but trying to actually do that yourself on the day without it looking contrived, along with all the nerves and everything else, can be really difficult.

I continued entering competitions like this right up until my early twenties. One big competition I entered when I was about twenty was called the Festival for Stars, which was a UK-based competition for which I qualified to represent Northern Ireland through the heats in Belfast. So I flew to Glasgow and did my performance. I didn't win, unfortunately, but I think I represented myself and Northern Ireland quite well. I also met a girl called Alice who performed on the night and was part of the judging panel that day. Little did I know I would cross paths with her again a few years later on *The Voice*.

CHAPTER 3

'WELCOME TO BEGINNER'S RUSSIAN'

I am very heavily influenced by traditional Irish music. Initially that would have been people that my parents listened to such as Mary Black and Frances Black, but also of course my aunt, Philomena Begley. At the same time, like most young kids I was always listening to the charts, too – anything from the Spice Girls to Boyzone and later Westlife. I was into all sorts of stuff across the generations. I just loved music!

When I was fifteen I had an amazing little taster of the music business when I went to see Destiny's Child perform live in Belfast and I actually got to meet them after the show. One of my uncles worked in the business at the time and somehow he was able to get some backstage passes for myself and my cousins. I had not that long come out of hospital from yet another one of my eye surgeries to try and reduce the high pressure. In this case I'd had some laser surgery so afterwards my eyes were really quite uncomfortable and sensitive. That meant it would be kind of a struggle at the show itself because of all the bright lights. But when I found out we would be getting to meet Destiny's Child backstage, it was such a big deal that I wanted to go, however painful my eyes might be. And sure enough I was lucky enough to meet them and say hello.

I spoke to Beyoncé and she was lovely; she asked me my name and thanked me for going to the show. I was so totally starstruck that I nearly forgot my own name! Don't get me wrong, we weren't hanging out in the dressing rooms or anything like that, it was really only a quick meet-and-greet, 'Hello, how are you?' type of thing, but that has always been a massive memory, fantastic. It's just one of those moments that you will always cherish (I saw her again a number of years later doing her own solo tour in Belfast and she was just phenomenal).

Straight after my A levels, I went to Queen's University in Belfast to do a degree. Initially I had wanted to do something with languages but as I got older I found it a bit difficult so I decided to study law and politics instead. I didn't want to study straight politics because I thought that maybe it would be more commercially viable to take law too, so that when I graduated I had the option to go down either route.

I really enjoyed that course. It was challenging, I'm not going to deny that, and there were some very tough times – especially with the law because obviously it is a such a text-based subject. I came across quite a few barriers just getting access to the material I needed to study. Although the university had had blind students in the past, they had mainly taken subjects like music, which were more practical, so I believe I was the first blind person to study law at Queen's. For that reason, it was a learning curve for both me and the university in terms of providing me with access to materials. The first and second years were a bit of a struggle but beyond that I really got into it and I enjoyed my university life.

I had a fantastic assistant at university called Marilyn. She was absolutely amazing, really helpful to me for three years. I also built a pretty good rapport with some of the tutors and the library staff – we were on first-name terms – so in that sense I got in there and built relationships to make my work easier.

I also began working for the RNIB as a volunteer for campaigns during my university years, trying to raise the profile of issues to do with visual impairment. That was an interesting development for me. Working with the RNIB in that capacity helped me to start mixing with other blind and partially sighted people, who I'd never really socialised with or, to be honest, even come across before. When I was at my mainstream school I was the only visually impaired person amongst 1,600 children, so I'd never really met anyone who could relate to my condition. So that was an interesting insight, and those people became a very welcome addition to my circle of friends.

Of course, university is not just about studying and academic life. It is a pivotal, transitional phase between your teenage years and adulthood. Suddenly you have to organise your own affairs, speak up for yourself, work out your own life and become self-sufficient. To a large extent, while you are still in school you are spoon-fed what you need to learn but at uni you have to learn to figure things out for yourself independently. There is not always someone there to hold your hand.

I wasn't exactly a hell-raising student, but I did have a great time and met a lot of friends. We had shared living accommodation in the second year with various European students from France, Spain, all over Europe and America too, and I still keep in touch with many of those people.

University was also a period when I definitely became more comfortable with my eyesight problems. I was much more confident explaining to people what it meant and what I could or couldn't do. So from that point of view I was becoming fit to articulate things that I hadn't done three years previously. I had kind of grown into adulthood and was a little bit more sure of who I was. University was definitely a big stepping stone towards that.

Perhaps inevitably, with such a love for music, it was always going to be the case that I would start to write my own songs. I've always had a pretty good imagination and I was quite good at writing back in the day – you know, comprehension in school and making up little stories and poems. As I got more and more into music, I always had an inclination to write songs and in my head I would come up with ideas, but I never actually found the right method for putting pen to paper. I tried to compose little bits and pieces on the piano but they never really came to a solid finish or a complete song. It was always something that I was fascinated with, though.

This was partly what drove me to take up the guitar, which I did when I was twenty-two. I just decided that I wanted to play an instrument again and I felt that because I had done piano for so long when I was younger, I wanted to try something different. I also had the notion in the back of my mind that the guitar was a better tool for songwriting; you could carry it from place to place, it was far more mobile and I felt it just offered me more possibilities.

So I took up guitar lessons in the evenings after work with a local teacher called Mark. To be honest, for the first year or so I really struggled because – a bit naïvely – I thought that if you learned one or two chords then, sure, you would be able to write like Mozart! I soon realised how mistaken I had been. Thankfully my teacher was very patient with me. I explained from the outset, 'Look, I can't see at all these days, I can't read music at all, so anything we do I will have to learn by ear and by memory.' I used to record the lessons and then go home and practise with my Dictaphone recording. For months I battled to try and make any decent sound out of the guitar at all. I suppose it was that bit harder for me because I couldn't play guitar tabs or read sheet music, which is an established way for a lot of people to learn. It was frustrating, definitely, but I just kept telling myself that anybody who starts off with an instrument struggles to play at first.

However, I suppose like everything else I have done before, I just stuck at it and through sheer determination I forced myself to keep going and keep practising, to the point now where, while I am no expert guitar player – by any stretch of the imagination – I am a lot better than I was when I started. I can muster a reasonable sound out of the instrument now, work a few covers and play along with my own songs.

I don't have a problem that I can't read sheet music or that I haven't learned the established technical approach to playing guitar. While I studied piano when I was younger by reading music, with my guitar I would always strum things out and learn by ear only. That approach has, I think, been very important. I knew that I couldn't read the musical tabs, so I just accepted that and therefore for me it was simply the easier way to go. Besides, I tend to agree with the school of thought that suggests that if you are overly technical, those very rigid guidelines can sometimes stifle creativity. I think that not sight-reading at all allows me to have a more natural and organic approach to music that I wouldn't necessarily get if I were reading sheet music. Of course, not everybody who reads music is a clinical and unemotive player; I would never suggest that. But I do think that learning by ear opens you up to creating very emotional and instinctive music. I genuinely feel that when I write a song I am emotionally connected to that piece of music because of this purely natural approach.

After I'd left university, I had started work in the civil service and it was really at that point that I found I wanted to explore writing first and foremost, especially creative writing. A friend and myself were thinking of going to an introductory ten-week journalism course at the Crescent Arts Centre in Belfast, which is a brilliant institution that encourages people, both young and old, to take up the arts, whether that be dancing, painting, music, sculpture or anything. One day I was studying the brochure online and lo and behold, there was also a twelve-week songwriting course. I just thought, *Right here we go, this is exactly what I want.* So I enrolled straight away.

Just before the songwriting course was due to start, I had begun to force myself to finish songs rather than just collate incomplete ideas, and as a result I had a handful of songs that I liked. So I was really excited to be starting this new course. By now I had been playing the guitar for a couple of years and so I had these few wee bits and pieces of songs but nothing major. I remember very clearly going into the class for the first time; obviously when I go somewhere like that I need to be guided into the class, so someone from the arts centre took me into this room and I sat down. I hadn't brought my guitar because I didn't know whether they would work with instruments for the first week, so it was just me. We all sat in there quietly and waited for the tutor to begin and when he did, he welcomed us all to the group and said he was looking forward to teaching us Russian for beginners!

The guide had put me in the wrong class, so as much as I would have enjoyed the opportunity to learn Russian, I figured I'd best say, 'I think I'm in the wrong place here,' and they managed to shovel me down the corridor into the correct room for songwriting. The guy who took that class was called Peter and he was really warm and informal, so he sat us all down – it was a bit like a therapy class! – and we all had to introduce ourselves. As the people said their names and a little bit about themselves, I thought, *Hang on here, is everybody else in the room male?* I must admit at first that was a little unsettling, because although it depends from person to person, a lot of songwriting can be quite open and honest, writing about emotional themes such as love, loss and all that there. You sometimes pour your heart out and I wasn't initially sure how I would feel in a room full of men. In fact, at the start of that first class I was pretty convinced that I wouldn't go back the following week.

By the end of the class, however, I could see that everyone was just kind of mixing in and doing their bit, coming up with ideas and lyrics, and it was very clear that we had a lot of common ground. So I thought, *OK, I am going to throw myself into the middle of this and away we go*. And do you know what? I never looked back. I loved every week and some of those people have become very good friends of mine.

Some critics might suggest that a structured class for something as creative as songwriting is a bit of a contradiction in terms. They might say it sounds a bit rigid and that you can't just make people learn how to write songs – it is something you either can do or you can't do. But for me, what that class provided was an impetus to set aside some time each week to think about writing and song ideas. It gave me a focus. It wasn't always necessarily the case that I wrote a song in the class, but I did always go home and make a conscious effort to be more professional in my approach. Before the class, I'd had the ideas in my head but I never had the tools to keep me focused on a weekly basis, to think about songwriting from one week to the next.

There were other benefits for me from that course, too. It had also given me a connection with other people of a similar mindset. We liked the same kind of things so we would often go off and work in informal writing groups together, to collaborate, and meet up quite regularly. The songwriting group also accepted me because of my interest in music – it was nothing to do with whether I could see or not, they all just accepted me as me. That was a great feeling. That whole environment just helped me to gain focus on what I was doing and during the twelve weeks (and a subsequent later course too) I felt like it all came together in the right kind of mix, in terms of progressing on the guitar, meeting people who had the same kind of ideas and interests, and fulfilling my desire to write songs. I was now totally into writing my own material.

CHAPTER 4

OPEN MIC,
OPEN MIND

By now, I had grown far more comfortable with my visual impairment. With the addition of my new friends from the songwriting group, I was lucky enough to have a very wide and varied social circle. I had my mates from uni, my songwriting friends and also various visually impaired friends too. By that point I was in my early twenties and I was comfortable with myself, whereas in previous years a lot of people maybe shied away from me and, indeed, I from them, because I still wasn't really used to the whole situation or happy with who I was, what I could or couldn't do, and also with explaining to people what my limitations were. However, as I got older I became more confident with myself, and those insecurities started to recede. I think it gets to the stage where you don't really care if people don't really like you or don't understand your condition.

I mentioned my visually impaired friends, but actually the irony is that for a long time I didn't really count any other visually impaired people as my friends. This was simply because I had been mainstream schooled and so I didn't come across any people my age with similar difficulties to me. I was the only visually impaired child in a school of 1600 kids, so although in one sense that could be very isolating for me, it also meant my friends were not visually impaired at all. It wasn't until I worked with the RNIB at university that I started to get some visually impaired friends around me too.

By this point, the combination of having sung for years and years, then playing the guitar and writing a few songs, then trying and loving that songwriting course, all meant that I was increasingly looking to keep moving forward with my music. The next logical step was to make my first public appearance performing my own material.

The impetus for this came from Mark, who had started off as my guitar teacher and had then become one of my good friends. He really encouraged me and said, 'There is no point sitting here doing all this music unless you get out there and start playing in public.' He suggested an open mic night that I had actually been to before as a member of the audience. It was in an Argentinian restaurant in Belfast; on a Tuesday they always had an open mic night so we made an arrangement for me to go and do that.

Although I had performed at all of those singing competitions in my childhood and was familiar with standing in front of a crowd, this was something totally new to me. It was very nerve-wracking, I don't mind admitting! Looking back I can see why my nerves were quite high – let's be honest, it could've gone down badly, especially in front of such a small audience. They could've thought, *This is a load of rubbish*, and maybe even have made those feelings known to me. I just had no idea how they would react to my performance. Sure, I had played my songs to my family and friends and, to be fair, my family would never tell me I was good when I wasn't, and would never have lulled me into a false sense of security. In fact, believe me, they would have been very blunt if they had needed to be! But at the same time, until you play your own material in front of a room of strangers who don't know you and who are just judging you solely on the basis of your music, then you don't really know what people think. I could have walked on to that stage that night and thought, *I can really sing*, only for those people to say, 'Er, actually, you can't.' That was a concern. To put your music out there to strangers and the public is a totally different challenge.

Mark played the guitar for me and we just did a couple of covers and one of my own songs. I didn't want to play guitar in public yet because I wasn't confident enough to play and sing on my own at that point. We did 'Rolling In The Deep' by Adele and a song of my own called 'January Song'. I absolutely loved it!

It was pretty simplistic as far as the show went, just a mic and the guitar, so thankfully from a practical point of view there weren't too many wires and there was no having to get up nightmare steps to get on to the stage area. It was really nice because the whole atmosphere was very much one of mutual support. A lot of other people in the crowd were songwriters as well, or were people who'd come down to hear their friend's music, so it was what I would call a 'listening audience'. It wasn't a case of people who were out for the night, wondering why there were these annoying people in the background making a bit of a racket!

I really enjoyed that very first open mic night and I got a huge amount of good feedback from everybody there. There seemed to be a particularly strong reaction to my own song, which was hugely satisfying. I felt the song itself wasn't bad – like I said, I am my own worst critic – but people were saying they really enjoyed it and for me that felt like a massive achievement. It was one of the earliest songs that I had managed to complete, so to perform it on my first open mic night and get such a good reaction was just fantastic. To hear other people compliment me and say they had liked the song and enjoyed my performance, especially on my first time doing an original song in public, was a brilliant feeling – a great buzz, fantastic. OK, it was only thirty or forty people in a small restaurant room, but that was enough for me. People also said my voice was amazing, both when I was singing the covers as well as my own material. They said it had a real clarity and authenticity to it, which was lovely to hear.

That open mic night felt very different from all the festivals and competitions I'd done over the previous years. I always really enjoyed the competitions, don't get me wrong, plus you often got great feedback from both the audience and the adjudicators. But those festivals just required you to sing along to backing tracks. This open mic night was a completely different test. It wasn't just about pleasing an adjudicator, it was about performing to an audience who were judging me solely on the music. There was no one sitting around with a pen going, '8/10 for diction and 9/10 for presentation.' It felt a bit more authentic. The whole vibe of the night was very different. It made me feel like I definitely wanted to do more of the same – I wanted to go out there and perform my own material again and again.

I don't know if I necessarily thought at that point that I wanted to make a career out of it, but I definitely wanted to have more of that sense of achievement I'd experienced that night. I loved being able to say that this song was something I'd created, something that I'd shaped from the beginning and put out there myself, and then being able to see it have an impact on people. I really wanted to write more songs and perform them in public.

I wouldn't say that afterwards I came home with a head too big to fit through the door – not likely, ha ha! – but it certainly gave me that little bit of confidence to think that maybe this was worth pursuing a bit more seriously. For several days after that debut gig, I was just getting sheer enjoyment out of my memory of the whole night, not to mention an overwhelming sense of achievement.

Soon after I did another open mic night and loved that too, then over time I plucked up the courage to play the guitar myself. I will never be an expert guitar player and I don't claim to be; I am still a learner – in a lot of things! However, I like the fact that I can put a couple of chords together and get a song out on stage and perform my own songs with my guitar.

I've generally had nothing but great experiences during these open mic nights. On a few occasions, I've been really proud because I have walked out in front of crowds that have been really noisy and disinterested and then I've sung one of my own songs and they've quickly started to quieten down, such that by the end of my performance the whole room would be listening in. That is a great feeling when you can do that. A lot of the time you are performing to other fellow musicians and people are pretty supportive, but you do go to some places where the crowd might not be as appreciative. You feel like you are trying to sing over the top of a hundred people shouting, but that is all part and parcel of the learning curve.

Of course, you also have nights when things don't go so well! There was one night when Mark and myself were playing an acoustic set with five other up-and-coming local songwriters in this downstairs bar in town. The problem was that getting onto the stage was a blooming nightmare, because it must've been two feet off the ground and there was no step up – a health and safety disaster for the blind! And, of course, as per usual I had quite high shoes on and I remember Mark saying, 'Just be careful coming off the stage, Andrea, it's quite a big step,' and I was like, 'Och, it will be fine, Mark.' Of course, when I came to walk off, with the entire room looking at me teetering precariously towards the edge of the stage, I nearly went flat on my face even though I was holding onto his arm. It really was one of those *You've Been Framed* moments – if someone had captured it on camera they would've earned £250 for sure. That aside, I have absolutely loved performing open mic nights and other small gigs out and about. I couldn't get enough of them.

In February 2012, my live experience was taken up several notches when I was asked to perform at the fiftieth anniversary concert of my Aunt Philomena. Fifty years in music – what an amazing achievement! There were numerous celebrations, including a big concert that was aired by TG4, the Irish language TV station. My aunt very kindly asked me if I would like to be involved because she knew that I also did a lot of Irish traditional singing. That was a massive opportunity for me. Although it was only a one-off TV show, the audience figures were expected to be really good because my aunt has a great following and is so well respected.

The concert at Newry Town Hall was actually was my first experience of TV, so it was fascinating. It was a pre-record so we were there for much of the day. I went down at about lunchtime. It was quite a large venue, with a capacity in the many hundreds. I recall they had a dressing room set out with all these chocolates and fruit and water, which was a bit of a novelty for me because I had never seen anything like that before when I had been doing my little singing competitions.

The whole day gave me my first insight into what goes on in terms of making a TV show: it was my first experience of going into make-up, wardrobe and hair, working with cameras, having a run-through and rehearsals. Now that I have been lucky enough to do *The Voice*, a lot of that stuff feels ... well, if not second nature then at least I know it is standard practice. But back then it was all completely new to me. I really got to see how much work goes into making a TV show.

It was such an enjoyable day and I was honoured to be involved and be there with my aunt to celebrate her fifty years in the music business. It was a really big event and a high-profile concert for TV, but even though she must have been quite nervous in herself, it never showed, and I was fascinated watching her command the stage, keep her performance at the highest level all night and behave totally professionally from start to finish. It showed me perfectly how those sorts of events should be handled.

Mind you, I can't say I handled it quite as consummately! I was seriously nervous. Not only was I singing *a cappella*, but I was also doing a traditional song in the Irish language. I speak some Irish but I'm certainly not fluent, so basically I was singing in a different language. I knew it was pre-recorded and that in the worst-case scenario they could do a retake, but this was my aunt's night and I really wanted to nail it in one take, to get the very best performance out of myself that I could. In the rehearsal I messed up the last couple of lines and I thought to myself, *Oh my God, if I do that in the actual performance it will be a disaster.* Then I just remember trying to calm myself down. It was quite a stressful time!

When I went out on stage I was still quite nervous but I managed to channel that and go for it and by the end of my performance I was very proud of myself because I had done the song in one take, I had sung something completely in Irish, I had performed it without any backing music, and it had been recorded for TV. The fact that I knew I had accomplished those things was quite a big personal achievement, for me to overcome those barriers. It was such a great night and I was so, so proud of my auntie.

Although it was filmed in February, the fiftieth anniversary concert wasn't due to air on TV until just before Christmas. By then, an awful lot would have happened ...

In the summer of 2012 – that turned out to be a really busy year! – I entered a show called *The Hit*. I was sitting at home one day fiddling at the piano, and Mum happened to be reading something in the paper and said, 'There is this new show coming out ...' and she read out to me what the purpose of it was.

The premise of *The Hit* was excellent, because they were looking for the best *song*, rather than the person performing it. So the focus was very much on the music. It was a pilot show and was due to be hosted by Laura Whitmore from MTV Europe. So it would certainly have a big profile.

At this point I had never been on TV (my aunt's anniversary concert hadn't yet been screened). To be honest, I deliberately shied away from any TV opportunities because I was always a bit concerned that people would maybe perceive my participation as, you know, blind girl, sob story, sympathy vote, blah, blah, blah. So I never really pushed myself towards TV, specifically because of that concern.

But *The Hit* seemed different. It was all about the song. There would be no focus on me as a performer on stage or how I looked. So I thought, *Do you know what? I might give that a go!*

So I did. I filled in the entry form and, of course, as per usual, I just got it in before the deadline. Then I went away and never gave the show a huge amount of consideration because I didn't think it would go anywhere. Then, lo and behold, a few weeks later I got a phone call from a member of the production team working on *The Hit*, who told me that my song – called 'The Message' – had actually got picked down to the final eight.

Then I learned that they'd had many hundreds of entries and also that the revered producer Steve Lillywhite was involved in judging the songs. When I heard I had been selected into the final eight, I was really proud. It gave me a massive confidence boost, I can't deny that.

In terms of my actual involvement with the TV show itself, it couldn't have been more different to what I would later experience on *The Voice*. We only really did one day of filming for *The Hit*, where each of the final eight songs were pitched to two artists, one of whom was Brian McFadden, formerly of Westlife, and the other was a band called Royseven from Dublin.

We did the day's filming in Dublin and it was actually just as I had come off my summer holidays.

So we had come back from a cruise in the Baltics and literally gone straight in to the recording of the show. I had to perform myself, but the emphasis was very much on the song – it was supposed to be nothing to do with the actual performer.

I enjoyed that day very much and really liked the concept of the show even more as a result, because for me it was about judging this song on its own merit, and nothing to do with me at all. From that point of view it was taking the whole visual impairment aspect out of the situation, as it wasn't focusing on the individual. I felt I had a great experience. The show was covered by all the papers so I had some exposure there and people seemed to be really into the programme. In fact, soon after the pilot episode aired and proved very popular, the show was commissioned for a full series, this time to be presented by Westlife's Nicky Byrne and the presenter Aidan Power.

My song didn't get picked as the winner but the very fact that it got down to the final eight and that Steve Lillywhite had heard it was a huge endorsement for me. Again it gave me that wee bit of confidence that, you know, *Maybe there is something in my songs, maybe it is worth pursuing?*

Trying to maximise my exposure on *The Hit*, I decided to contact various radio stations. *The Hit* had only been a one-off screening but it had still got my name out there, and built up a little bit of recognition. I made contact with a girl called Lynette Fay who coincidentally had gone to my secondary school, though she would have been a bit older than me. She had started to work as a DJ a few years previously, initially on an Irish-language programme, and because she was very successful she had gone to work on other shows, including one on BBC Radio Ulster. By pure chance, she had been at the fiftieth concert for my Aunt Philomena that I had appeared at back in February and she was very complimentary about my performance that night. Not long before *The Hit* was aired, I did a local event in Pomeroy during a weekend of traditional music and Lynette happened to be there for that too. So when I contacted her again after *The Hit* had aired, she was really supportive. We arranged for me to go into her radio station the week after.

I had only ever been on the radio once years ago as part of a local Children In Need event I had done, singing a little song on my own, so this was my first time to be on air solo as an adult, performing one of my own songs, playing guitar and singing live. It was BBC Radio Ulster too, so this was big pressure. You might think that doing all the open mic nights and gigs would've helped me with nerves but, to be honest, this felt totally different. I was sitting in a radio studio with just a few people nearby, playing and singing live, knowing that it was going out to however many thousands, or hundreds of thousands, of listeners around the country. I have to say I was feeling the nerves. As I was performing, I was thinking, *Cripes, if I make a mistake, there is no going back, this is live on radio, no second chances!*

However, I managed to keep a hold of my nerves and I really enjoyed the whole experience. Hannah came with me which helped and it was just really good fun. Looking back, teetering on that knife-edge of knowing I could not afford to make a single mistake was sort of appealing. In a weird way I think I must get some kind of kick out of that intense pressure!

Mind you, halfway through the song I did start to do something that often happens when I'm performing live, and it's something I have since found out that other singer/songwriters and performers do too. I started to have a conversation with myself.

'You don't know the words to the second verse, do you, Andrea?'

'Och, sure I do …'

'No, you don't, and it's coming up really soon … are you gonna forget the words there, Andrea?'

'No, I know them, it's fine …'

'You wrote the song, how can you not know the words?'

'I'm fine!'

And so on! It sounds crazy but I had this conversation while the song was carrying on; fortunately, on that day at BBC Radio Ulster and indeed on nearly all my subsequent performances, I have rarely forgotten the words. So despite the voices in my head, it's been OK!

A lot of the music that I write, I often just used to keep it stored in my head. That probably sounds weird but it's because I use my memory so much, for the most part I keep a lot of stuff in my head. That to me is a natural storage space. All songwriters will be similar, in that once you create a song and play it over and over as it evolves, the piece will naturally become embedded in your mind. But perhaps I relied on that more than most, because I don't have the luxury of going and reading things that I have written down. I could type the ideas all out but the songs just flowed out of me and it felt more natural to store them that way, rather than clinically sitting down and typing things out.

However, as the quantity of songs grew, there developed a need to put things down and record them, initially using a Dictaphone or my iPhone. I have a great circle of friends around me who help with my music and so, for example, Mark, my guitar teacher who'd helped me on that first open mic night, would record material on his computers, using programmes like Garage Band. Other friends did the same for me too, such as Jim, Dave and Adrian from the songwriting class, especially if we'd collaborated on new songs. So there were snippets here and there that we had recorded to help us remember them, but there was nothing too formal.

However, as my love for songwriting grew, I wanted to do some more structured recording. I wanted to get the songs in a nice format that people could listen to, that I could pass to radio, just for them to have a listen and see if they thought there was any merit in trying to put my music on air. Essentially I thought, *Right, well, I am not going to go anywhere with this until I have a half-decent recording of my songs!*

Mark had a friend called Dave who worked in a recording studio and they invited me down there for a couple of days. This was around the same time I was getting ready for my aunt's fiftieth anniversary concert, back at the start of 2012. We kept things very, very basic; it certainly wasn't a case of hiring a twenty-five-piece orchestra! Mark played the guitar, I did the vocals, and another friend of Dave's played a little bit of piano. There were a few other wee bits and pieces, but essentially that was that. Exceptionally basic but that's what I wanted.

We did three songs, all original material of mine, and I was really pleased with the results. The quality of the recording was pretty decent too, even though it only took just a couple of days.

I was still very new to the music industry at this point, however, so – perhaps typical me! – I kind of sat on the recordings for a wee while. I was uncertain what to do with them, to be honest. Do I send mp3 files out? Who to? Or do I produce a physical CD? In my defence, I was working full-time and at this stage I had started to do a part-time postgrad course in law, plus I was still doing all the open mic nights and playing gigs too. So I had a fair amount on!

Mark was great, though. He said, 'Andrea, you really need to do something with these songs – we recorded them in February and it is some time since, and you still haven't really done anything with them.' So along with Mark and a friend called Fionuala, we came up with a strategy. The plan was to get the recordings pressed into physical CDs, get a cover designed and arrange an EP launch.

I wouldn't say I was actively looking for a record deal at this point. Now, I suppose maybe in the very back of my mind I thought it would be nice if someone picked it up, of course, but I was mostly looking to test the water and see whether people enjoyed my songs and my voice.

I knew that people from around where I lived liked my stuff, and also I got a good reception at open mic nights and gigs or when playing at home to friends, but beyond that point – namely when it came to a mass audience – I didn't know if it would work. So as much as anything, I think I made my debut EP just to establish if there was any interest in my music. The EP launch was arranged for mid-December and in the meantime I got myself busy pressing the CDs and getting the artwork ready.

Then, out of the blue some time in August, I was Facebooked by my friend Geoff who had helped me at my very first open mic night where he had been the master of ceremonies. He said a production team from *The Voice* was in town scouting for people to audition for the show … and he thought I should try out.

CHAPTER 5

THE VOICE BEGINS

I was, of course, well aware of *The Voice*. I had seen the first series and I liked the show and the coaches. Perhaps more than most people I particularly loved the fact that the contestants were being judged on their voice only. It wasn't all razzmatazz and image, it was purely about the music, and I'm sure I don't need to explain why that was such an appealing prospect to me! Most other shows inevitably judge you on what you look like, and not just how you look in terms of physical appearance, but also in terms of how you perform, assessing you on how you move about and your facial expressions or whatever else. That has never really been my forté as an artist. Of course, my visual impairment is a contributing factor but being more sedate on stage is generally just my nature as well – I am not really flamboyant in terms of performance. So there was a huge appeal to the show from that point of view; it seemed to be offering a unique opportunity.

However, when Geoff Facebooked me that day, I wasn't really sure what to think of his suggestion. I didn't know whether going on *The Voice* was right for me or not. In the past, the thought of entering various televised music competitions had crossed my mind, but apart from that appearance on *The Hit*, I had never really given it massive consideration. So I was intrigued but not sure what to do. I sent Geoff a message back asking for some more information about it and he gave me their email address.

I didn't email them straight away. For a while there I pondered what to do, swinging back and forth in favour of, and then against, trying out for the show. On the one hand, I was thinking about pursuing my EP and working on my own songs – I had the launch night all arranged by now and my CDs were being pressed up, so maybe I should just keep plugging away at that rather than go down the TV route, the so-called 'fifteen minutes of fame'? On the other hand, it was a huge TV show, and was very credible because of its focus on the vocals. And if I did OK and progressed through a few rounds, it would give an incredible boost to my profile.

However, it was a risk. What if I failed? What if the experience destroyed my confidence? I could've very easily just folded up and said, 'No, I don't want to touch any of that TV stuff,' and carried on doing the open mic nights and my EP and all that. I would have really enjoyed that too; I would have loved still doing music, even without the prospect of millions of records or having my songs sung by people all over the world. Whatever had happened would not have stopped me from loving music, from singing and performing, because a fundamental part of the appeal is just doing what I love, enjoying music for music's sake.

Then I started to feel that despite these reservations, *The Voice* offered me the most amazing platform to showcase my singing and also my own material. Even though the show itself was all covers, with no original material being permitted, progressing through a few rounds would nonetheless provide the most amazing step up in my career. If I did well, it would surely provide an opportunity to devote more time to music?

Then the real world reminded me of a few practicalities. Obviously I had a full-time job, plus I was doing a Masters degree in law and governance. In addition, I was doing my little gigs and songwriting and the open mic nights too and in many ways I felt very comfortable in that environment. In one sense I didn't really want to upset the apple cart. I was also aware of how incredibly hard it is to make a living from music. I looked at other friends around me in my music circles and they were really struggling to make enough money. It is not easy. By contrast, I had a good, reliable job with prospects, so in a sense music was a luxury for me and I knew I would really struggle to live off the proceeds of my music if I left my job. I'm not talking here about all the trappings of fame like big houses and fast cars (not that a fast car is a fat lot of use to me!). I'm just talking about being able to pay your rent, go to the supermarket and buy some decent food. I was thinking about just making a living, surviving.

However, it was clear that *The Voice* was also very focused on developing people as artists ... so that made me swing back in favour of entering ... and round and round I went, trying to figure out what was the best thing to do.

It was a total conundrum really.

Eventually I decided to go for it. *Who knows, maybe I could get through to the televised blind auditions? If I could just get to sing in front of the coaches, that would be incredible.*

The work that goes into *The Voice* before it gets anywhere near being televised is just unreal, it really is. These teams are sent out all over the UK scouring the country for the best unsigned talent, and the producers audition people for months and months before any of the televised blind auditions. People work so hard on that show.

One of the ways they look for potential contestants is to contact open mic nights and acoustic gigs all over Britain, tell the organisers they are in town and do they know anyone locally who would be worth looking up? Hence Geoff deciding to Facebook me. They also do open auditions too, so it really is a very thorough and time-consuming process.

Eventually, after all my procrastination, and I admit with a wee bit of trepidation, I contacted the guy from the production team of *The Voice*. We swapped a few brief emails and I thought, *Right, I'm going to go down and have a chat with them and see what the vibe is like.* So that's exactly what I did. At this point, the meeting with *The Voice* team wasn't even really an audition. I had arranged to see the man I had been emailing at a Holiday Inn in Belfast city centre where they were based. We had a brief chat and he seemed like a really nice guy. Then I literally sang a couple of lines from 'Make You Feel My Love' and that was that, I left. Before I left he spoke – again very briefly – and seemed impressed. He said he felt I should consider filling out the full application form and officially entering for the show.

When I got back home, I started going over all of the pros and cons of entering again. I wondered what were the consequences for me if I did this, if I filled in that form? Then again, what were the chances of me doing well on *The Voice*?

I was still unsure what to do at this stage. Somehow doing that very brief initial meeting at the Holiday Inn had brought it home to me even more that I was pushing myself into the TV arena, which is a big decision to make. And I'm not a rash decision maker, I will weigh up all my options, and think, *What is the best plan here?* That's just my nature. But in the end, I thought, *Just go for it, Andrea, see what happens, give it a shot, there is nothing to lose.* So I decided to fill in the form. I did that and got an automated reply saying the application had been accepted and that they would be in touch.

Not long after, I received another email with a date and time for a more formal 'first' audition in front of the production team. It was at 8.30 at the same Holiday Inn in town. I spent all day preparing myself, getting ready hours before the allotted audition time. I went on my own and didn't tell anybody apart from my friend, Mark, who helped me with the initial email, and my sister, Hannah, who helped me fill in the full application form. Even then I swore them both to secrecy, because I really wanted to see what happened before I mentioned it to anyone else.

Some people have asked me why I didn't tell anyone – in fact I told hardly anyone for months to come. I suppose I kind of wanted to test the water before I said anything. Plus, I've learned in the past to play my cards close to my chest until I have something to say: there was no point in talking about it until there was something to talk about, if you get my meaning. So that was my approach and in fact I stuck with that through a large part of the early stages of the show.

Anyway, back to the night of the first audition proper. I got there in good time, I was well prepared and felt reasonably relaxed. At least I was relaxed until I got to the reception and they told me that my audition had been due at 8.30 *in the morning*! I was twelve hours late!

Fortunately the guy on reception was really helpful and he escorted me up some stairs to the audition rooms. He knocked on the door but lo and behold, no one answered. The room was empty, locked up. *The Voice* people seemed to have all gone home for the night.

He said he would go and have a look around the hotel to see if he could find anyone from the show. All the time I was thinking I had totally blown my chances, it was really embarrassing. Eventually he found them all gathering downstairs in the foyer, putting their coats on and their work stuff away, ready to go and have dinner and shut up shop.

The guy from reception said to them, 'Look, there's your girl here to audition,' and they were caught a bit off-guard, I suppose. They very politely pointed out that the auditions were supposed to have finished hours ago. I explained myself to them and why I was twelve hours late, but I felt totally ridiculous, I just assumed I had completely wasted the whole opportunity. I'd heard about these sorts of shows and if you don't turn up at your allotted time they just turn you away; they have so many people to see and get through that they simply can't afford to make alternative arrangements. So I figured I was finished before I had even started.

However, the guy from *The Voice* was really nice and he listened to my explanation then went off for a couple of minutes before coming back. 'Listen, we are going to see what we can do …'

That was so accommodating and immediately put me at ease, because I thought, *This is a really nice set-up, these are really nice people.* He went off looking for a conference room for us to step into momentarily and shortly after he returned and guided me through a door. He'd set up an iPod to sing along to and I sang a verse of Sarah

McLachlan's 'Angel' (most people mistakenly call it 'In The Arms Of An Angel'); that song would come to play a very large part of my time on *The Voice*. I couldn't really see whether anyone else was watching me but I knew there were a few people there. Mind you, to be honest, I was that far gone with all the events of the day – being late, scrabbling around trying to find the staff from *The Voice*, then trying to concentrate on what I was singing – that I didn't really take everybody into my notice.

When I finished singing they seemed really quite impressed, and thanked me for coming down. They had a very quick chat with me, and told me they couldn't yet say one way or the other if I was through to the next stage or not, but that they would be in touch. Despite them all being so nice, I honestly just assumed that because I was so late I would have no chance of progressing and I pretty much figured that they'd let me audition out of courtesy. *There's not a chance in hell*, I thought to myself. Funnily enough, straight after the audition I went and did a gig in town, an acoustic night that had been booked in for quite some time. So it was a busy night!

A while later, I got another email from *The Voice* team that said, 'Right, we would really like to see you again but this time it will be a more formal audition in London.' I will be honest and say I didn't really know the process so at this point I initially assumed they meant this would be the audition in front of the four famous coaches, but it soon became apparent that in fact this was another audition in front of producers, behind closed doors.

So I phoned my sister Hannah and said, 'How do you feel about flying to London with me to audition for *The Voice*, ha ha?!' Throughout this whole process Hannah has been there with me, because fortunately she was usually available to help out. (My little sister Lucy who is seven years younger than me was not always available so much, unfortunately, because she was at uni doing exams and quite often there was very little notice about travel arrangements and so on. Plus a lot of the filming was midweek so she was in lectures and classes.)

I was obviously really pleased to get the call to fly to London, but at this point I also figured that there were likely to be a heck of a lot of people still left in. So I didn't get too carried away. As much as I thought there was always a chance to do well, I didn't really believe that I would be fit to make it that far through the process.

Then they sent me a request asking for different types of songs for me to sing – slow songs, mid-tempo and uptempo numbers too. I worked on that and it was OK apart from the faster songs because I don't really sing many of those. I managed to come up with a long list and fired those through and thankfully the songs they chose were 'Angel', Texas's 'Say What You Want' and 'I Won't Give Up' by Jason Mraz.

You might be wondering how I managed to keep all of this from my parents – to be honest I'm not entirely sure! It was with great difficulty, actually. I didn't want to say anything yet in case it all came to nothing so Hannah and I said we were just going into Belfast for the day. I can't remember the exact story we made up but we didn't say anything about London, obviously. And because we were going and coming back in the one day we could say that and be believed, so we went incognito and hoped that nobody spotted us.

We made the trip to London and I arrived – on time! – for the producers' auditions. This was in a room with various members of the TV team who I would later get to know very well as people, but at that stage to me they were just producers of the show and so the environment was all pretty unfamiliar. There was some initial chitchat, and then they explained the process to everybody ... the most striking aspect being that if you were to get through these auditions then you would be travelling up to Manchester next to audition on the TV in front of the four famous superstars!

On the one hand that was a very exciting prospect but, as I have said before, I am naturally a cautious person, so I didn't want to get ahead of myself. As much as I was taking notice of what they were saying, another part of me thought, *Well, is that likely to happen? Really?* It's a weird kind of feeling because as much as they are informing you about the next part of the process and what you need to do and what will be required of you in terms of time and travelling, the other part of your brain is going, *I might not even get to that point.*

I haven't had any more knock-backs with my music than anyone else. I've obviously lost competitions and things like that there, but I wouldn't say I've had a shocking amount of rejections either, in the sense that any competition I've gone into, I've generally done OK in them. Some of them I have won, some of them I have come runner-up, some of them I haven't done so well.

With a TV show such as *The Voice*, I think you have far more reason to be cautious. This wasn't a local competition, this was a huge national TV show which I later found out had over 30,000 people audition for it. As much as I knew there was always a possibility of doing well, and I certainly seemed to have impressed them in Belfast, I didn't know how much everyone else had impressed them as well. Plus, when you go to that level, things step up a gear. That's not to take away from the local competitions because there are a heck of a lot of talented people in them who would not necessarily enter TV shows. However, when you step it up to a UK-wide TV level, you are competing with people who are professional singers and professional musicians. Music was something that I knew I had a talent for but it wasn't my job. In terms of stage presence and performance at my local gigs, I would have still been fairly lacking in confidence. Whereas I suspected a lot of the other people entering *The Voice* were doing that every night of the week. That was their bread and butter. It later transpired that some people may have had previous record deals in the past and some were performing nightly in West End musicals, so for those contestants this was all second nature. From that perspective, I still felt I was very much a novice, just starting out. Testing my way, just seeing how far I could go. Of course, there were a few people on the show who had less experience than me and naturally they were probably looking at me and thinking similar thoughts. I wouldn't say that was a negative outlook, I'd say it was realistic. Everybody looks at their own achievements in a different light. Therefore, taking all of those things into consideration, I felt my caution was well placed. *Really, what are the chances ... ?*

Anyway, I did the callback in London and they seemed to really like my performance of 'Angel'. It was quite comical at one point, though, because before my audition, I had met a brilliant vocal coach from the show who was really into having the right posture when you sing. Now I am really terrible for this – I have the world's worst posture, I just slump over. Anyway this vocal coach had given me quite a few tips in the warm-up, but then when I was midway through my song, she ran up and started to pull my head in different directions and push my shoulders about! Obviously it wasn't particularly easy for me to see what was going on; all I knew was that someone was pushing and pulling me about mid-song! *What is this woman trying to do to me?* I soon twigged that she was helping me with my posture, but at the time it did feel quite awkward. If anyone had taken a photograph, it would have looked absolutely horrendous, but it was done with the best of intentions.

Despite this, my performance seemed to go down quite well. They also asked me to sing a traditional Irish song to demonstrate my Celtic roots, which I did *a cappella*. They seemed to enjoy that too and one of the producers said my voice had a very authentic feel, which really made me feel good. Again though, I didn't know whether they were simply offering me pleasantries or whether it meant they genuinely liked my vocal. It can be difficult for me to judge these things as I can't see facial expressions and I can't really tell from body language at all. Therefore I have to go entirely on people's tone of voice, which is the only kind of insight I have on their true feelings. And even then, people can speak in one way but be thinking another. I really don't have any visual cues, you see, so it can be very hard to read a situation like that.

I was pleased with myself, though, and I walked away thinking I had done a good-enough audition. I was happy to go home and say I reflected myself in a good light and if it worked, it worked, but if not then so be it, I had done my best. So me and Hannah went back to the airport, flew home and again didn't tell anybody.

A while later, I was at work when I noticed I had a voicemail. As per usual I'd missed the call because the mobile reception at work is pretty horrible and the signal dips in and out. I listened and was shocked to hear it was someone from *The Voice*. I knew they were not going to tell me on voicemail if I had got through or not and, sure enough, they asked me to call them back. My initial thought was one of excitement because I figured that if it had been negative news they might have just emailed me. So I went out of my office and made the call.

'Andrea, I'm delighted to tell you that you are through to the final 150 people to audition in front of the coaches for the TV show.'

I was so thrilled, it was just the most amazing news!

I just instantly felt like it was a massive achievement, just to get to the point of auditioning in front of those superstars. It is such a tiny number of people who get through to that stage compared to the 30,000 who audition. That's a heck of a lot of people. So I knew it was an absolutely massive achievement, and regardless of what might happen next, I was very proud.

That exhilaration lasted a few minutes and then suddenly, *WHOA! What do I do now?!* The realisation hit home that I was going to have to travel to Manchester, stand up on stage on TV in front of four massively famous faces and a big studio audience, as well as gosh-knows how many millions watching at home, and perform a song. Reality started to kick in, I suppose.

It was a very surreal phone call to take. As I've said, I'd only told a couple of people prior to this. No one knew at work so I had to just go back to my desk, calmly sit down and carry on with my job. While trying not to think of Will.i.am, Danny O'Donoghue, Jessie J and Sir Tom Jones.

It wasn't until I'd got this final 'yes' from the production team to say that they would like me to audition in front of the coaches live on TV that I actually told my parents and my younger sister. To be fair, I had tried a few times to make the announcement at home but the longer I left it the harder it seemed to be to broach the whole subject. A day or so after I had found out, I was visiting my parents and we were sitting down to tea together.

'So, do you know that show there, *The Voice*?' I asked my mum.

'Yes, the one with Tom Jones and all that?'

'Yes. Well, I auditioned for it a wee while ago and there's like thousands of people who went after it and they've whittled it down and ... well, they want me to go on the telly and audition in front of the coaches!'

They were pretty pleased!

They were also a little cautious too, because as parents they wanted to be reassured about the possible repercussions on my life if it went well, or equally if it went badly. So we chatted a wee while there and discussed what might happen if it backfired, or if I managed to get further in the competition. They hadn't been aware of all those initial auditions, remember, so it was a lot to take in!

Apart from my immediate family and the couple of friends I've mentioned, I continued to keep the secret for quite some time, because I didn't want everyone to know just in case it ended up going not so positively. So in the coming weeks, I had the odd day off work here and there using up my holiday time and I think most people just thought I was off doing my Masters. They never got remotely suspicious!

In the background to all of this crazy stuff with *The Voice*, I was still working, still studying for my Masters, still doing my live shows around Belfast and, most importantly perhaps, I was grafting hard organising the launch party for my debut EP. Oddly, my EP launch night turned out to be just a week before the 'blind audition' at the BBC's Manchester TV studios. So I had quite a lot going on!

The launch party for the EP was 13 December 2012, at a place called the Menagerie in Belfast. It went really, really well. I got Mark and a few of his friends to set up this wee band and we played the songs from the EP and a few other tunes too, plus a few covers. A lot of my friends and family came down and it was just a great night, a showcase for all that I had done over the past two or three years. I really enjoyed myself.

I was also hoping to make a few pounds back from selling some CDs, ideally to go towards the cost of pressing them up. I think I sold them for three quid, and we did sell quite a few, so that was also very encouraging. But that wasn't the main point of the night, of course; it was all about showcasing my original material, performing those songs in front of people and trying to take my music to the next level.

It was also quite a strange night in the sense that I had all this stuff with *The Voice* going on in the background. I'd done those producers' auditions and had been back and forth to London to meet the team ahead of my blind audition in front of the coaches, but most of the people there that night knew nothing about this. So it was almost like I had two separate but parallel strands of my life going on at the same time.

Less than a week after my EP launch night at the Menagerie in Belfast in front of a few dozen friends, family and local music industry people, I flew to London to walk on stage and sing in front of Danny O' Donoghue, Jessie J, Sir Tom Jones and Will.i.am.

CHAPTER 6

'HAS ANYONE TURNED AROUND OR NOT?'

As I set out from home to head to my first-ever performance on *The Voice*, I was totally excited. *Whatever happens, this is going to be brilliant and, who knows, maybe I could get past the blind audition round?* It was ever so slightly nerve-wracking too, though! It was a hectic few days to say the least. The programme was filmed at MediaCityUK in Salford, the BBC's new flagship headquarters. Hannah came with me and, after transferring from our flight, we checked into our hotel and unpacked. Obviously it can take quite a while for me to get my bearings and feel relatively comfortable in a new environment, an unfamiliar room, not knowing where anything is at first. It can add to my stress, I suppose, although I am pretty used to it by now. At home I can motor about in my own environment reasonably well with my cane or if I'm in an unfamiliar environment I can ask someone and they can guide me around. But something like flying to a hotel in Manchester, then having to spend several very hectic days in a TV studio is a very alien environment (for anyone), so I always needed somebody with me. Most hotel rooms are actually quite standard and in a couple of minutes you will find the stuff you need, but usually I have a torment to (1) find the shower and (2) figure out how to switch the shower on without scalding myself, then (3) discover where the heck the towels are kept! If only I had a pound for the amount of times I've had to ask Hannah, 'Where are the towels?' The other classic is toilet roll which, how can I put this ... well, you very quickly learn to check it's in a reachable place before you start your business!

This might all sound like a bit of a nightmare that I could have done without that week, but to be honest it was just fine. I've had these sorts of challenges all my life, and I see them as just general irritations and frustrations that I am completely used to. It was definitely magnified because of the enormity of knowing I would be appearing on *The Voice* and because we would ultimately be moving in to different hotels all the time, but in Manchester the room quickly became semi-familiar to me. It can feel quite restrictive because I'm not as free to move about in the hotel as much as I might want, but it was not a big deal, really. I actually enjoyed the chance to get some sleep ahead of my blind audition, so I did spend quite a lot of my free time in the room.

We headed over to the BBC and straight into our first meeting with the production team, where we had some initial chats about how the next few days would pan out. There were to be numerous rehearsals and prep before the actual filmed audition in front of the coaches. We went to see the studio itself and I don't think it was until I walked in there that the gravity of what I was doing actually sank in. This was *The Voice*!

On the day of the dress rehearsal I felt reasonably fine. I'd had the chance to work with the band, practise my song and familiarise myself – as much as I could – with my new surroundings. The studio was a complex maze of corridors, cables, steps, stages and cameras, all the paraphernalia that goes with filming a major TV show. So I was having to get used to all that as well as focus on my performance, but it was fine. We also met the vocal coaches and I picked up a fair few tips there, too. It was all very exciting and I felt my dress rehearsal went reasonably well. I was very happy with the band and with the track, 'Angel'; I liked the song and I was comfortable with it, which I think was half the battle. I knew the words backwards and it felt right for me. So I was glad in a sense because I had enough stuff to worry about without doing a song I didn't feel 100 per cent relaxed with.

In between the dress rehearsal and the actual audition, me and Hannah went and did a bit of shopping and my family came over for a couple of days too, and we hung out together. That was really great, a good distraction – it helped me relax and I tried not to think too much about what would be happening shortly.

There was such a mix of emotions swirling through my head. There was always this duality of thought, so that as much as I kept convincing myself that no matter what happened it was already a really big achievement, another part of me was thinking about what might happen if it backfired. And specifically, now that I was at the studio and around the whole mechanism of *The Voice* with the coaches' chairs and those four red buzzers, one thought kept creeping into my head: *Cripes, what if no one turns round?*

That would be seriously embarrassing. As much as it would have been a vindication of everything that I had done up to that point if someone did turn round, it would have been hugely humiliating if nobody did. I couldn't imagine how much that would have knocked my confidence. Singing in front of four superstars, a big studio audience and millions watching at home? Wow!

How amazing! But then imagine all of the above seeing no one turn around for you? Ouch. Disaster!

I had met a few other contestants before the filming night, but only briefly at either the original callbacks or during the dress rehearsals. However, because of the numbers – there were still about 150 people left at this stage, remember – there wasn't really much of a chance to get to know them or even find out how experienced they were coming into the show. So I couldn't have really said at that point that I got to know any of them all that well, it was just brief chats. You don't really hear each other's rehearsals either, so you don't know what your competition is like.

One aspect of those first few days on *The Voice* that I didn't enjoy at all was my first interview! Looking back I feel so sorry for the guys behind the camera, because I was being my typical, evasive civil servant-esque self and I was giving them all these really boring answers that basically revealed nothing at all. Everything I said was noncommittal, and it made me sound like a bit of a robot, really dull. So they were gently trying to coax a more interesting answer from me, repeating the questions while I was sitting there uncomfortably, thinking, *Why have they asked me the same question twenty times?*

In my defence, there was an element of not wanting to talk too much about my visual impairment. They obviously wanted me to talk about that part of my life and I found it … I wouldn't say 'difficult' … because I don't generally find it difficult to talk about any more. I used to, back in the day when I was kind of adjusting to the whole thing, but now it doesn't bother me to talk about it and I can explain to people what the condition is and what it means I can and can't do. I love to take the mickey out of myself, too, and people close to me know this and we have a great laugh with it. But in those first few days of *The Voice*, I found those questions quite tricky. I was more self-conscious about my visual impairment, not because of the condition itself, but because I was wary of how that might come across on TV. I was worried that if I was seen to be talking about this on the show and I wasn't saying exactly the right things, then it could come across as a plea for a sympathy vote. I suppose that was one of my key reservations – how I would be portrayed as a blind person on a reality TV show – because you could be walking yourself into all sorts of potential problems. My intention had always been that I was there for music, 100 per cent. At the same time, *The Voice* is a TV show, it is a story, and viewers buy into the lives and personalities of the contestants. It would be naïve of anyone to think otherwise. So I knew that I would have to talk about my visual impairment and that this was a perfectly fair line of questioning. That didn't mean that I was totally comfortable with it and I knew I had to choose my words carefully and with tact. However, I quickly realised that the people behind *The Voice* were not in the business of capitalising on my visual impairment; they clearly weren't trying to sell me as a sob story. At the same time, they needed to reference the fact that I had a visual impairment and that I couldn't see the coaches and – most pertinently of all, perhaps – *that I wouldn't even know if they had turned around for me or not.*

This was a genuine problem. When I went into the dress rehearsal, they asked me if the coaches were visible to me, and I said, 'Well, look, if the coaches turn around' – 'if' being the operative word – 'I will hear the noise as they press their buzzers, won't I?' You know, that big 'swooosh' as they press the red button and their thrones zoom around.

Apparently not! The team explained to me that the noise is actually dubbed over after the show has been filmed, and therefore at the time of my performance, there would be no audible indication that one of the coaches had turned around. Of course, the audience would most likely cheer if that happened, but the crowd were cheering on and off throughout the performances anyway, so that was certainly no way to gauge if a coach had turned around. When I heard them explain that, I thought, *I am really in trouble here. I am just not going to know.*

I was really concerned because it could potentially be so embarrassing and awkward if I had to ask if anyone had turned around. So I deliberately tried not to think about it, but just to focus on my singing and performance. I told myself, *You are here to sing: just go out there and do your very best and worry about the coaches after that.*

I'm not sure if it was stress or just a genuine cold, but the night before my audition in front of the coaches, I was as sick as a parrot, I really was. It's the whole story of my life, throwing huge amounts of vitamin C down my neck before a big performance – I always seem to get ill right before an important show or audition. I guess from that you could say it must be a stress thing, rather than a coincidence. But it's never a good time to get a cold, whatever the cause! Hannah and me went to the chemist shop nearby and we must have bought up their entire stock of cold remedies – anyone coming in after me was doomed for disappointment! We had bottles of medicine, Lemsip, vitamin C, paracetamol, fruit-flavoured lozenges … anything that was vaguely thought to help with a cold and sore throat, you name it, we bought it. I was a walking pharmacy!

Suitably medicated, I headed for the actual performance in good time on the Tuesday – not twelve hours late this time! By then I was really feeling my nerves but I was also very excited and fully intending to totally showcase myself and do a good job. That was a long, long day; I needed my adrenaline that day. It started off really early, first thing in the morning. The way they worked it was each audition day had one morning and one afternoon session to work through the contestants in turn, but even though I wasn't on until the evening session, everybody was required to be present all day. They had to do filming of you walking in to the studio, interviews, chats with the vocal coaches and all that, so there was loads to do while you waited for your performance.

When I arrived they first got me into make-up and hair, which at that stage was just a very quick once-over because there were so many contestants that they couldn't afford to spend a whole lot of time on each person. Then we were wired up ready, so there were microphone packs hanging here, wires hanging out there. We also had an initial chat with Reggie Yates (who was presenting the show with Holly Willoughby) in the morning, which was filmed, and that went pretty well. I just chatted and I found myself feeling fairly comfortable talking to him. Then after some more interviews and prep, we were told we could go out for a wee while as they didn't need us for a short time. Mum went to the shops, Hannah and me went for a bite to eat at Harvester's and Dad ... well, he went on a tour of Old Trafford! Then it was back to the hotel briefly before heading over to the studio for my performance.

At this point in a very long day, I felt weirdly calm, quite at ease in fact. The whole atmosphere was really friendly and comfortable and even with all the TV people rushing about and cameras going off everywhere, at that point it didn't bother me too much. I later wished that feeling of tranquility had persisted because when I actually got to the stage I became really, *really* nervous.

Unfortunately, by the evening time when my session started, I didn't feel very well at all. By this time, the one thing that I found the most distracting, even disturbing, was the buzz. There was just so much going on, this real cacophony around me. Obviously I couldn't see what was creating so much noise, but it was just everybody else, the contestants chatting, some people singing part of their song, runners and production people rushing about, walkie-talkies chattering into life, snippets of music blaring out from the sound system, vocal coaches working with

At my christening with my parents and godparents: Plunkett Begley, Kieran Begley, Ann Begley, Andrea Begley and Sinead Boylan.

In my christening gown, still enjoying a relatively 'normal' life at this point.

Around eighteen months old.

On a pilgrimage to Lourdes after having developed my juvenile arthritis.

Singing with my aunt Philomena Begley. They literally couldn't get me off the stage!

In hospital after major eye surgery in London, with Brownie the Bear. To help prevent them feeling alone, children were encouraged to bring along a teddy who would go through the same operation.

I've always been so lucky to have a very close relationship with my sisters Lucy and Hannah.

Celebrating Aunt Mamie Begley's birthday with sisters Hannah and Lucy.

On my bicycle.
Despite my on-
going health issues
I continued to have
a normal enough
childhood and was
full of energy and
enthusiasm.

At my Holy
Communion.

On my first day of
Primary School.

As bridesmaid to
my cousin Nuala
McCreesh (née
Begley) for her
wedding, at eighteen.

Meeting Destiny's Child with family and friends. We were so nervous and silly around them. All my sister Hannah could remark was, 'They have arm hair!'

At my Formal with cousins Maria Jordan (left) and Mary Jordan (right). The dress, the limo, the boy …

With my brilliant classroom assistant Maeve at my A level prize giving. I achieved three A grades and won my school's top score in Politics, coming third in Northern Ireland for that subject.

At Festival For Stars.

At my graduation from university. I achieved a 2:1 in Law and Politics.

Singing 'Angel' by Sarah Mclachlan at my Blind Audition.

Team Danny just before Battles.

people, staff popping in and out, sandwiches and crisps being snacked on … there was just so much background noise. While I know some people find that kind of white noise comforting, for me it was all spinning around in my head while I was trying to concentrate on my thoughts, and I found that quite distracting. Eventually Hannah and me took ourselves off to a quieter room and immediately that felt better.

Luckily my cold had mostly subsided by now. To be fair, it was never really a full-on cold but it had had me worried there for a wee while. I was conscious of it, although perhaps more conscious of the *thought* of it than anything. I still had a bit of a scratchy throat but I suspect it was mostly psychosomatic. Plus I'd had so many vitamin tablets and cold remedies by then I don't think any cold in the world would have survived!

As my turn approached, another contestant walked into the quiet room that me and Hannah had hidden away in. I'd been enjoying the peaceful atmosphere and was starting to calm down, but this particular contestant was absolutely rigid with nerves. She actually got so worked up that she started crying in front of us, which didn't do a whole heap of good for my own nerves! She was just a living manifestation of pure fear. Hannah tried to comfort her and gave her an iPod and said, 'Just listen to the music, take your mind off it,' but she was very upset and seeing her that way made me think, *Cripes, as much as I am sitting here telling myself don't worry, I am absolutely panicking now!*

External you wouldn't have guessed I was getting so edgy, because as much as I get anxious before a big performance, I am not really the type to cry as such, so while I was nervous within myself it wouldn't necessarily be obvious to other people. However, as the time ticked by, the worse my nerves got; although oddly there were also times when I would drift into a state of relative calm only for it to then hit me again, BANG!

Then it was time to move up to a holding room where there were only ten or so people inside, and I could feel my turn creeping ever closer. I was taken in for a very quick couple of minutes' interview, right before I was due to go on stage, asking how I felt, what were my thoughts and so on. And this blooming holding room was like a greenhouse! It was so incredibly hot, with all the lights and cameras and not much ventilation – it was just a sauna. It was the hottest I've ever been in my life, I thought I was being grilled alive. I wasn't even in there for that long but the sheer heat was awful.

When that was done and dusted, I went in with a smaller group of people who were being held in another room, then the vocal coach took me to a side room to give me a quick briefing before I went out on stage. He mainly asked me if I had any concerns in terms of the song and the words. I didn't; it was just all about whether my nerves would get the better of me or not. He was great and we chatted for a wee while there, and I told him exactly how I felt – which in fact was a view that I held for my entire *Voice* experience: 'Whatever happens, whatever the result will be, if I walk out there and do a performance that I can say sold myself in the best way possible, then I'll be happy. It may not be what they are after, it may not be what they deem good enough, but at least I will feel that I have done myself justice, and put 100 per cent effort in. That is all I can ask of myself.' He said, 'Andrea, you will smash it.'

I remember having a real last-minute 'I have to go to the loo!' nervous pee, then shortly after someone came and took me off to the side of the stage. At that point I knew that Jessie, Tom, Danny and Will were literally just a few feet away from me. I couldn't see them, obviously, but I wasn't alone in that. None of the contestants had seen any of the coaches at this point; we were kept strictly separate. Obviously with the show placing so much importance on the coaches not seeing the contestants, this was vital and I have to say *The Voice* team were incredibly strict about this. They clearly wanted to keep the process as pure and as honest as possible. Even to the extent where the coaches' dressing rooms weren't anywhere near where we were; if one of the coaches momentarily used a particular corridor, they would lock it down, so that there would be absolutely no possibility of walking into one another. They were brilliant like that.

'Right, Andrea, you are up next.'

I actually felt pretty horrible with nerves when I heard those words, it was just such an extreme situation. I couldn't see the audience or the coaches from the side of the stage, so I was really trying to second-guess what was going on. For some reason I could also hear this really weird, droning bass sound: it was awful, a horrid, unsettling noise that completely went through me.

Of course, trust me, I had a big pair of heels on. One of the production staff was guiding me and it wasn't his fault but as he helped me over a cable ramp I didn't really step on it properly and I wobbled terribly. That made me feel even more nervous: *Oh no, cripes, I can't even stand up, this is not good.* There were a series of steps to navigate on to the set itself, but thankfully I managed to get over all of those. I felt like I was moving in slow motion as he guided me up on to the stage. We walked forward, then the chap from the production team gently placed me in the right position and handed me the microphone.

OK, here we go.

I could sense the audience was big. I couldn't see them but I could tell it was a large room. I had asked the day before what the capacity was and I'd been told it was about 700. That alone was bad enough, never mind all the cameras and on top of that the four famous coaches sitting somewhere in front of me. Standing up there alone, all I could see was a few lights, that was about it. Everything was really hazy. In the dress rehearsal I could see slightly more because the lights weren't turned on properly but at the actual blind audition, the studio lights were turned on fully so I could hardly see anything at all, it was just a blur.

To be honest, that didn't figure on me – I was concentrating so much on what I was doing that I never even really bothered to look or to try to see anything, because I just thought there's no point in me attempting to focus on anything here because that's only going to distract me. I couldn't even begin to see the coaches. Again the dress rehearsal had taught me that I wouldn't even be able to see the chairs they were sitting on so I figured why waste energy trying.

In the interview before the performance, I'd pointed out that music was my natural get-out from life's difficulties, and I said that singing really 'takes me to somewhere else, somewhere that is totally cut off from reality ... I just feel a complete sense of relaxation, and it is something that I can just automatically do without needing any assistance or having any issues.'

So there, standing on the stage, riddled with nerves in front of the coaches and the audience, with millions watching at home, that's what I said to myself.

Just sing.

I opened my mouth to sing and the first words flooded out. Instantly, as soon as I started, the nerves caught me straight away. They almost took my breath away. Normally when I perform there are always a few jitters, that's only natural, but nowhere near to this extent. I could feel the anxiety getting worse and worse and worse, rising up in me, really strong. Only towards the end did I feel a little bit more comfortable with it, but for most of the whole song I was nervous ... *really nervous.* There was so much at stake.

I was going over the whole day in my head while I sang – that contestant breaking down in tears in the quiet room, that awful din in the studio, my own nerves swinging from sheer terror to a strange calm. It had been such an extreme day.

Come on, get it together, this is really important.

I wasn't waiting for anyone to turn around because I knew that I wouldn't be fit to see or hear them anyway, so for me the essential thing was to get to the end of the song and do a decent job and then worry about the rest of it when it was all over. It was just ninety seconds of pure concentration, performing, remembering the words, keeping a check on the nerves bubbling up, doing my absolute very best to make it count.

I know now from watching the show back that Danny turned around very quickly, in fact only about twenty-five seconds after I started singing. If I'd have known that, I certainly would have relaxed and been able to enjoy my performance a lot more! When he turned around, the crowd applauded but then at the time I didn't know that it was for me; part of me guessed that maybe that was a good sign, but I didn't know for sure. As it was, I just had to get to the end of the song without the knowledge of that, just holding myself together until the end. When I had nearly finished, the crowd applauded quite a lot and again, after the event, I found out that that was when Tom turned around. Then when I finally finished – yes! – they applauded for what seemed like a good amount of time and at a decent volume, I thought, but again, you just never know. I thought it was probably just because I had come to the end of the song.

I still wasn't fit to know if anyone had turned around or not. I hadn't a clue.

For my part, it was just a big sigh of relief that I had got through it. Having said that, I didn't really feel that I'd performed the best I could. I had given it my all in that I was fighting all the way through against my nerves, but I didn't think it was the best performance I could give. I felt the nerves had really got in on me and that there was more to my performance potential than that, I could really have sold myself better. It did improve as the song progressed, but I wasn't totally happy, to be honest. I was just so relieved to have got through it, given the fact I was almost incapacitated with nerves.

However, once I got to the end of the song, the weirdest thing happened, because I suddenly felt so much more relaxed. I think it was simply because I had got through it all and hadn't collapsed! That performance was just massive, massive pressure, and the worst of it was self-inflicted: *Don't mess this up, don't make a disaster out of this, calm yourself down, you have got to deliver here*. The scale of personal expectation I put on myself was immense. I felt it was an amazing opportunity to perform to four superstars of the music industry, a massive audience in the studio and at home. Even if no one had turned around, maybe you could look back on it in years to come and say, *There's the time I performed on* The Voice.

So by the end of the song, as I say, I felt major relief, and then I started to feel a lot more relaxed. As a result, I suppose the talk just flowed out of me! In the moment, I guess my own natural reaction worked OK.

Danny asked me my name and where I was from, then said, 'What's your background?' And you can hear on the clip that I pause ever so slightly before replying, 'I'm twenty-six and I work as a civil servant.' Well, actually I was twenty-five at the time and straight after the audition my mum said, 'Why did you make yourself older?' Well, it was because the producers had pointed out to us that the shows wouldn't air until the following spring, so if your next birthday was before then you needed to make yourself a year older for the purposes of the broadcast.

I wasn't thinking about my age, mind you, I was wondering if anyone had turned around. In my head I was like, *OK, how exactly do I broach the subject here? You might want to chat to me, Danny, but did you actually turn around? I don't want to be blunt but seriously? ...* That was pretty much what was running through my head. *How do I phrase this without sounding very abrupt?*

So I just said, 'I'm also visually impaired so I'm not entirely sure whether anyone turned around or not!'

Of course, the audience could see what was happening next but I couldn't. All I heard was some brief applause then next thing I know, I can hear Danny from The Script (he'll always be Danny from The Script to me) standing right next to me and saying gently in my ear, 'I absolutely turned around, that was absolutely beautiful, wow, gorgeous. Really, really amazing.'

It was such a strange moment; the first of many that day. I was like, *Seriously? Did that just happen?* It was the most surreal thing I have ever experienced in my life. I hadn't even seen Danny before that moment. I'm a huge fan of The Script so I'd seen them in concert but that doesn't exactly prepare you for him standing next to you whispering in your ear. Honest to goodness, it was the weirdest thing, totally out there. I never ever expected that.

He went and sat down, and I laughed and said, 'Well, that's a relief!'

Then he said, 'I can assure you not only we turned around – myself and Tom ...'

Oh my God! Tom as well?! That was the first I knew of that!

'... but the whole of the UK just turned around too.'

Then he asked me what inspired me to go on *The Voice* and I just explained that it was 'for the very basic reason that you couldn't see me and I couldn't see you,' which seemed to raise a chuckle, then I continued and said, 'and for once I am on a level playing field with all the other contestants.'

Next thing I know, I hear Tom Jones, music business legend, introducing himself to me! He said he was unsure at first because he felt I was most likely to go with Danny, but he said, 'I couldn't help myself because your voice is so beautiful and I just had to let you know that and I would love it if you would be on my team and I would work my guts out for you!'

By now I was in a bit of a daze really, it was just so weird, but so fantastic. Jessie said I should be proud of being so courageous and complimented my voice. Will's comments weren't broadcast but he was generous too and just politely said he felt I needed a little more control in my voice. At the time I agreed with him but I knew that was because I was nervous – it was not an unfixable problem.

Then it was a case of concentrating on what Tom and Danny were saying, because that was my choice. They were both trying to get me on their team. Never thought I'd see the day. Mind you, although they didn't broadcast this bit, I thought I would get a cheeky hello here for my sister Hannah who absolutely loves Tom Jones. She's a massive fan. I thought, *You will never get this opportunity again*, and it's not normally like me to be so forward, but I thought, *I wonder if I can get Tom to say hello to Hannah? This could be my cheap Christmas present!* So I just straight out asked him: 'Tom, is there any chance you could say hello to my sister? She is round the back with Reggie, watching it on a big screen and she's a big fan,' and he was lovely, he said no problem and did exactly that. Although that was edited out, it was brilliant – Hannah was just going nuts in the other room, she couldn't believe he'd said hello to her.

Tom then went on again, 'I think we both feel very emotional about the way you sing,' and Danny was agreeing with him. Then it came to Danny's official turn to speak: 'My gut instinct is I always kinda, go with my ears, and what I feel but there's one thing that doesn't lie and that's the hairs on my arms and I've used that as a test throughout this whole thing. I could coach you impeccably. You know, excellence is what this team is all about. Your song choice is impeccable. The emotion that you sang with is exactly the same emotion with myself that I have strived to try and get and also to look for in another artist. I really, really believe you have it. It would be an absolute honour for me, cos I think I'd be in the arms of an angel in fairness if you were on my team.'

This was getting ridiculous now!

Then he added, 'I might be going out on a limb here, but you are Irish ...'

I couldn't resist a quip back: 'Oh, no, not the Irish card ...'

I heard some more laughter and then it was time for me to make my mind up. It wasn't broadcast but I said to Tom and Danny, 'What do you think you could do for me?' Apparently Hannah and Mum nearly fell over when I started to question them: 'You don't start to question Tom Jones and Danny!' But I had to see who was going to do the most for me. I was just being diligent!

By now I was laughing inside at the sheer absurdity of it all. I think to a certain extent I had been buying myself time by getting Tom to say hello to Hannah, because it was all so unexpected. Up until that point my expectation had been that if any of them turned around, the person I would've wanted to pick was Danny. Just because I felt in musical terms ... not that I am saying I write like The Script ... but I suppose in terms of my general musical direction, the ways that I write, being a singer/songwriter, the songs that I wanted to sing – they were all in a similar vein. Plus I was a Script fan; I loved a lot of their songs and I really liked their style of writing. That's not to say that I don't like Tom and Jessie and

Will's stuff too, because I do, but in different ways. I just felt that Danny was the person I could learn the most from. And perhaps also the one who would appreciate my material the most. That was my initial thinking. This was all whirling around my head as I stood there on that stage.

But then when he told me that Tom had turned around too, I genuinely did start to think, *Hold on a second here, I need to give this a bit of consideration, this is my one and only opportunity to decide between – wait for it – Tom Jones and Danny O'Donoghue!* I really didn't want to make a rash decision. *Tom has been in the business for a long time, he's a legend and he knows a heck of a lot about things, so maybe I should go with Tom because he is the more experienced one?*

I probably mulled over the decision for a minute or two on the stage, I was kind of flitting between the two of them, but then I went back to Danny because that was my original thinking. My gut instinct.

'I'm going to opt with … Danny!'

I later found out he jumped to his feet and punched the air with both hands then he came up to me for a hug – weird moment again – and turned to the crowd and was orchestrating their cheers: 'Give it up! Come on!' All the coaches came on stage to chat to me and I thanked Tom for turning around and said, 'I think you are absolutely fantastic.' All the time I was chatting with the other three, Danny was whipping the crowd up: 'Give it up! Wow!'

Just the most surreal moment of my life, there's no other way to describe it.

CHAPTER 7

PARALLEL LIVES

At the end of the blind audition, one of the floor guys came and helped me down, then Danny walked offstage, and I was like, *Seriously?* I remember stupidly saying, as I was coming down off the stage with 'Danny From The Script' (he'll always be Danny From The Script to me), 'Oh no, I shouldn't have worn these heels. I am not exactly helping myself – blind and in five-inch heels, not really a recipe for success.' But my excuse is my head was in a total spin!

I went and met my family, which was obviously filmed too. They commented on how nervous I had been and they were all delighted that Danny and Tom had turned round. Hannah was going crazy because Tom had said hello to her. That was such a stark contrast: one minute I was being hugged by Will.i.am, Danny, Tom Jones and Jessie J, then next I was talking about it with my family. Such extremes of emotion and experience.

I've always watched these shows and seen people say how you forget the cameras are there, and I always thought, *How on earth can you forget the cameras?* But genuinely, when there is that much going on, so much excitement and adrenaline and chaos, you do forget them – you are so lost in the moment that you don't really think about what is going on around you, all the film crews and the TV people, or how you will look on camera.

After that I had to do a quick interview with *The Voice*'s web team, then there were some briefings with the production team about when they would need me back again – for example there would be a contracts meeting a few days later – and all sorts of other stuff to organise. When that was all done, we were allowed to leave and then – suddenly – I was standing outside in the street, with just my parents and Hannah, almost as if it had never happened.

'Er, well, shall we just go and have some dinner then?'

It was nine o'clock at night and it was weird, because after that amazing night, we found ourselves sitting in a perfectly normal restaurant, having a general chitchat. Obviously no one else around us knew what had just happened. It was such a bizarre feeling. We spent the entire meal completely deconstructing what had gone on and talking about everything. The full post-mortem.

'Can you believe … ?'

'Oh my God, how about when he said …'

'Did he really do that … ?'

Then the very next morning, after struggling to sleep from excitement, it was straight to the airport, on a plane to Belfast, quick stop at home to drop off bags and so on and then … back to work.

So after all the craziness of London and the blind audition, I suddenly found myself back at work, sitting at my desk, surrounded by all my usual bits and bobs, answering phone calls, sending and receiving emails, trying to work as normal, but all the time just beaming to myself and going over the incredible events of the day before.

We were not supposed to tell anyone about the audition, because it wasn't due to be aired until the following March, so no one at work knew. As my work friends came up to me during the course of what to them was a perfectly normal day's work, it was so hard not to say anything. I would be talking about something that needed to be done but all the time I was thinking, *You wouldn't believe who I got a hug from last night!*

The following days were a bit of a haze, because I went back to my 'normal life', meeting friends, working, doing my Masters degree and my music. Then I had to snap out of all of that and fly back to talk about some legal stuff with *The Voice*'s production team in London.

That was also the very first time I had the opportunity to meet all the other people who had got through the blind auditions and into the so-called 'Battle Rounds'. I managed to have a chat with a few of the other contestants in my team, but it was only brief. I recognised some of the people from being around them in passing during callbacks and on the audition day itself, but most were strangers to me. There wasn't a huge amount of opportunity to mingle and get to know each other at that point.

I didn't see Danny From The Script on that trip. I wasn't sure how it would play out or when I would see him next, but I totally anticipated that with it being the Christmas holiday period that everybody would be off for a wee while. After that legal meeting was tied up, I just went back home to Pomeroy again and finished work for the Christmas break on the Friday and then had a lovely, normal, family Christmas, as you do.

I still didn't tell anyone; it was literally just my family and the two friends who had helped me get the first meeting through Facebook who knew about it. I was very conscious of the fact that we were not supposed to talk about it. That said, there was another reason I kept quiet too. Whereas before I was uncertain if telling people might set me up for embarrassment if I failed, now that I had got through the blind audition I was worried I might jinx myself if I went round telling people. Everything was going really well, so I worried that if I suddenly opened it up to a bigger crowd of people, it could fall apart. In some stupid way it did feel like the more people I told, the more I would bring about bad karma on myself.

No doubt about it, that whole period was a weird time. I was living in these two completely parallel but unrelated universes, switching from *The Voice* and celebrities and TV then straight back to my normal day-to-day life as if it had never happened. It was very unsettling.

All the drama surrounding *The Voice* did indeed die down for a few weeks over Christmas but I obviously still thought about it. The memories would hit me in waves – I'd be doing something at home or work and then, BANG! I'd remember Tom Jones talking to me or Danny From The Script hugging me. A few times I would hear a Script song on the radio and that was a very strange feeling, knowing that in a few weeks' time I might be in a studio somewhere working with Danny. I was *so* looking forward to that!

I was still doing my music in and around Belfast, of course. Just after Boxing Day I had a gig at a place called the Sunflower Bar in the city. That was my very next performance after singing on *The Voice*, and it couldn't have been more different, just an acoustic set at a small but great little bar in front of a modest crowd. It was a completely different experience, but I loved it all the same. I was still promoting my EP and doing live performances, really trying to focus on that side of my music, but I have to be honest and say all the time in my head I was thinking, *Cripes,* The Voice, The Voice, The Voice*!*

By the middle of January, there started to be quite a lot of traffic from *The Voice*'s team – emails and phone calls organising my next trip and informing me what was happening in the coming weeks, and admin stuff like clearing permissions to use personal photos when they broadcast the little film about me on the first show. It's a tricky job for the team – they are trying to build up a picture of you and your character so that the viewers can feel some kind of connection with you and get to know you a little bit better as a person. Of course, you are never going get to know anyone through two-minute VT clips all that well, but it's just to give a flavour. And they have to do that for every contestant – it's so much work! To make a TV series like *The Voice* look effortless, there is an incredible amount of hard work going on behind the scenes, a staggering amount in fact.

The next big thing to get through was a day that had been set up for me and the other members of my team to meet Danny. I was quite excited about that, *obviously*, but the more cautious part of me was a little bit worried. Why? Because I'd seen some of these shows before and sometimes these days out and excursions involved ice-skating off a cliff somewhere, or bungee jumping off the side of the London Eye, that sort of stuff.

Don't get me wrong, I can be spontaneous and do some crazy things. I did white-water rafting when I travelled to Peru in 2010, and I really enjoyed that. I was scared beforehand, obviously, but I thought, *To hell with it, I am going to throw myself into this!* It was so much fun. They were not extreme rapids but it was bad enough for me, someone who is not exactly the world's biggest thrill seeker.

However, in the environment of *The Voice*, I wouldn't have felt very comfortable doing something as extreme as that. So before the meeting with Danny, I was worried, thinking, *Cripes, I really hope it's not going to be some activity that I am going to totally struggle with, that would be a bit pants.*

Fortunately, that wasn't the case – it was just a day meeting Danny and it wasn't being filmed, so it was just a genuine chance to get to know him a bit better, albeit in the presence of the rest of his chosen team. We were told we were meeting Danny at a private members bar – come on, private members bar, please, oh, do you? I'd never been in one in my life. The plan was that we'd have a bit of food and a chat, so I was much more relaxed with that. It was also an opportunity to have a chat with everybody else who had got through the first round. I naturally migrated towards a contestant called Conor who was also from Northern Ireland, and I also really liked Laura, Abi and Paul. I found out what everyone's background was and their motivation; some people had tried out for shows before and other people were professional musicians and already constantly gigging, making a living from music. Some wanted to give it a try to see whether they could get a record deal and go that bit further. It was a real mixture.

There were a few people from the production team but not a huge number, so we pretty much had the whole downstairs room to ourselves. There was loads of food – burgers, sandwiches and crisps. Now normally you can never hold me back from eating but on that occasion I was just completely gone on the whole 'Danny From The Script factor', so I just nibbled a couple of things.

Danny was really good. When he first came in, he went around the whole group and remembered all of our names, saying hello and having a little chat. He remarked to me that he has a sister called Andrea and that made my name memorable. He stood at the side of these comfy sofas where we all were and just talked to us in a normal and natural way. He threw in the odd curse word and made us laugh too, putting us all at ease very quickly. I didn't actually expect him to be anything else, to be honest – I didn't expect him to have an air of celebrity or a sense of aloofness. You never hear that said of Danny. I kind of got the vibe from him that he was just an ordinary person and, yes, he was famous and a well-known face but in himself he was very down-to-earth. From the get-go that's exactly the way he was with all of the group.

He said we had all done fantastically well to even get to this stage. He then explained his own band's long and at times arduous journey through the music business, about the years that they'd worked in America with little or no reward, and how they had more or less given up before they'd earned their breakthrough. It was fascinating. I think from the very beginning he kind of put across the message that you are not going to get too far in all of this if you don't put in the hard work. As much as we all know that is the case, to hear it first-hand from someone so successful was really important. That was the key message that I took away from that meet-and-greet day.

The only part of the day that I disliked was when we had to watch back our auditions, collectively. I was absolutely cringing. To be fair, everybody cringed at their own performances, as you do, but as each singer watched on in horror, the rest of us sat there going, *Cripes, that is our opposition – that is pretty scary, they are amazing!* So as much as we were all critiquing ourselves, we were also observing our competitors. That reminded me that I was in a competition; up until that point we had all been picked to get to the audition stage alone, and it felt a lot more like an individual process. Then I realised that the next time I was going to go out there to perform would be in a Battle and one of us would be going home. Not that I didn't expect an exceptionally high level of competition on *The Voice*, but to see those people in person and their performances made the competitive aspect of the show sink in much more.

Danny mentioned that he'd actually been on holiday over Christmas and he told us it was the first proper vacation time he'd had in four years, which made me think, *Gosh, seriously, is that the music business?* What we also soon realised was that Danny is *so* dedicated, such an incredibly hard worker. For example, this is how dedicated he can be: before that meet-and-greet, he'd actually gone on YouTube and looked up all of our songs and performances that were posted up there, not the ones we had done on *The Voice*, but all our own personal stuff from before the show. He'd obviously spent hours watching and listening to the clips of all these dozen or so contestants in Team Danny, to get a better feel for what we could do as artists and to inform himself before he picked our Battle songs. Then it became apparent that he had done this research while on the first holiday he had managed to take for four years. That tells you a lot about the man, right there.

Mind you, as he was telling us about YouTube and all the clips he had seen, it dawned on me, to my horror, that the main clip of me available online wasn't exactly very flattering! *Cripes, please tell me he hasn't seen the one of me singing covers in a shopping centre.* I had gathered together some other clips of myself doing much more credible gigs and I had been full of good intentions to post some of those on YouTube, but I hadn't managed to quite get them up before Christmas. So the only real video was this shopping-centre gig where I was singing 'The Climb' by Miley Cyrus. It isn't a bad song but obviously I felt I'd developed much more as an artist since then, not least because I had been playing guitar and writing my own songs.

There wasn't a huge amount of one-on-one time with Danny but I did manage to get a very brief chat with him at the end of the day's events. Lo and behold, as Hannah and me were talking to him and I mentioned a few of my more recent clips that were now on YouTube that I much preferred, he said, 'Oh, yes, I did see the one of you singing covers in a shopping centre!' No!

He left then and we all gathered our things up and started to make our way home. When we came out of the building, Danny From The Script was standing outside having a smoke. We had to wait for someone who was collecting us to take us to the airport for our flight that evening, and while we were there, Hannah told me that several women and girls were walking past the building entrance and just staring at Danny, almost walking into lamp-posts, literally hitting their heads doing a 360-degree spin, just not believing that it was him.

That was just a very small example of his celebrity and it made me realise what happens when people start to recognise you. I suppose to a much smaller extent I get that now, but from my point of view I'm not aware of it because I don't see it! Unless somebody tells me or walks up to me and says, 'Are you the girl from *The Voice*?', I don't get to know about it. I guess Danny is used to it but hearing about it that day was a little bit of a reality check.

After the meet-and-greet, we went back home, once again straight back into normal life. It was my birthday weekend just after and even at this stage I still hadn't really told an awful lot of people. By the end of the month things started to heat up, though, and we went back over to London again to be filmed with Danny's guest coach, Dido.

Before that, we were all lined up and filmed for the big reveal about who the Battle Round pairs were going to be. When Danny called out who I was singing against I was worried. I was paired with a singer called Alice who was absolutely lovely: beautiful, a really nice girl and an amazing singer. I knew Alice very vaguely from before the show because she had been involved in the Festival for Stars competition in Glasgow that I'd taken part in a few years' previously. I definitely remember her performance that night singing a Whitney Houston song, and I did remark that she had a lovely voice. My sister Hannah later told me that Alice had since been in *Hollyoaks*, so it was clear that she had enjoyed success and would definitely be a confident and strong performer.

To be absolutely honest, at the same time, I also thought that it wouldn't have mattered who he picked for me to sing against, because I felt that I probably didn't have a chance regardless. To make matters worse, Hannah had told me Alice was a good performer and was able to move around with great stage presence, no doubt due to her acting background, so that was a big concern. She had all of that to bring to the table and I didn't have anything: it was just my singing.

The second worry was that I didn't know the song we were given by Danny for our Battle, which was 'People Help The People' by Birdy. I'd heard a few bits of Birdy's stuff before but unfortunately I didn't know that particular song at all. So now I was feeling the pressure of having to compete against a performer who I knew would have a big stage presence, and also I had to learn the lyrics and melody of a song I wasn't at all familiar with. Obviously I can't read the lyrics from a piece of paper, so at home I would normally just sit with my iPod for hours going over and over the words until they sank in and became second nature.

However, when you're in a time-constrained environment like *The Voice*, it is a totally different story. As soon as I got out of the room where Danny had paired us off, I was determined to learn the words perfectly. The schedule was for us to go in and perform in front of Danny and Dido, so no pressure then! I think I also put a lot of pressure on myself to learn the song as much as possible, probably because I knew the team were more than happy for people to go in front of Danny and Dido with lyric sheets, because they didn't expect them to learn all the words in that relatively short period of time. For me that was no use because I couldn't read. So I really had no other choice but to learn, or try to learn, the words. I just completely immersed myself in the song for a couple of hours, had some food, went back to the song again, and just got it into my head as much as I could. We weren't allowed to leave the studio because it was all being filmed in the one day, so it was a pretty noisy environment but I just tried to shut everything out and concentrate.

Alice was in the same position in that she didn't know the song either so the both of us were trying to learn melody and lyrics at the same time. I am lucky in that I have always had a good, reliable memory so all I kept doing was playing it over and over on repeat through my headphones, listening and listening and listening. Then one of the team came and explained that we would sing alternate lines, which made life a little bit easier because it meant I only had to remember the lines that were relevant to me. This was also the first time I got to meet Ali, one of the vocal coaches, who in the end became my vocal coach the whole way through the show; he was great and had so much charisma and energy.

It was just as well I did work so hard on the lyrics and melody because within about three hours of being told the name of the song we had to learn, I was in a recital with Dido and Danny standing on the other side of a piano. It was really intense. For one thing, I never thought I would have the opportunity to meet Dido, so I was thinking that even if I didn't get through the Battle Rounds it was still exciting that I had had the privilege of singing for her. Alice and I went up to the rehearsal room and walked in to see Dido and Danny standing there. That's a moment to remember. We weren't able to speak to Dido that much; pretty much most of what was said you can see on the broadcast. You can't rush in and say, 'I am a massive fan and I love *White Flag*!', which is what I would've loved to have done.

We ran through the song a couple of times and I was happy with how it went. I felt that my performance came across quite well, which I was shocked by because we had had such a short time to learn the song.

Because Alice had been concentrating on learning the melody, she hadn't had much time to learn the lyrics so she was still reading them off the sheet, and that wasn't really benefiting her because she was spending more time trying to concentrate on reading the words. So that was quite hard for her. By the end of that rehearsal I was quite pleased; I felt, *Well, maybe I've got a shot at getting through here*.

Danny wasn't really very critical of anything I was doing – he seemed to be pretty content with it but then I didn't know whether that meant he was disinterested in my performance perhaps. He was also giving Alice tips about her harmony, so maybe the fact that he was giving her more advice meant that he would rather see her go through? It was very hard for me to read the situation. The longer I was in the competition, the more I stopped trying to read too much into things because I just didn't know. I just tried to focus on what I could do from my side, because to try and start second-guessing situations was wasting my time. In that room, he also said to us, 'Look, I haven't made my mind up in advance, I really haven't. It will be a case of who performs best on the night, because I have to see whether the nerves get to people and I have to know whether you can handle it on stage in front of the audience when it really counts and the cameras are rolling.' I was happy with that, because it meant if he didn't choose me I would still have been able to walk away and say, 'To be fair, he said he would look at his decision on the basis of the performance on the night and if I just didn't come up to scratch in his opinion then fair's fair.'

After that there were more interviews to do; I was becoming a little more comfortable with that part of the process now and I think my answers were much less robotic. That was quite a gruelling day – there was a lot on with several interviews and stuff happening backstage, yet it was all so exciting. I was still new to the whole TV world and unfamiliar with how everything operated, but in terms of the staff there, I started to feel much more comfortable and relaxed. I soon began to see them more as people rather than just as part of a production team. You spend so much time with them, it is an intense environment and there is a lot riding on it, so we developed a real camaraderie, which was comforting and helpful. Crucial, in fact.

At this point I definitely was hoping to get to the next round. My main goal was actually to be able to spend more time working with Danny; at this stage there were thirteen people in his team so the opportunities for one-on-one work with him were very limited. He was involved with us all, but because he had so many to look after, he obviously couldn't dedicate as much time to each individual as we might have liked. I knew that the next round would involve half as many people and so I would logically have far more time working with him in person. That was really what was pushing me and driving me to fight on.

After we had done some press photos, I do remember at that point having a bit of a chat with Dido, complimenting her and saying I really liked her songs and that I thought she was a great songwriter. She very kindly complimented me on my voice and I can't deny it was wonderful to hear someone like her say that. I was starting to realise that the celebrities we were working with were just people. OK, they are exceptionally talented individuals but at the end of the day they are also just normal people and you begin to see this when you interact with them one to one. Of course, at times you do pinch yourself and think, *Oh my God, I am standing here talking to Dido.*

Danny was chatting with me too; I said that I seemed to be catching planes as if they were buses, and he warned me about that, telling me that aeroplane air-conditioning was one of the worst environments for your voice. He was like, 'Make sure you drink loads – hydrate, drink plenty of water, a ridiculous amount of water!' I said, 'Never mind being guided, if I drink the amount of water you are suggesting I will probably need a catheter on stage!'

By the time of the filming for the Battle Rounds, I was really quite friendly with Alice so it was a strange feeling knowing we would be up against each other. Potentially the other singer could put you out of the competition.

It's an odd kind of conundrum because on one side you are working with the person and trying to learn the song together and for both of you it is important that the performance is good. However, ultimately there is only one spot available in the next round. At the end of the day, if you try to dominate the other person it probably won't do either party any favours because the audience will see that, so it is important that you gel with the person and that you sing together, resulting in a good joint performance.

Danny advised us of exactly that. 'Remember, this is a Battle but ultimately it is also a great advertisement for your singing. Obviously do your bit and try to shine but don't overdo it; don't shout at each other.' Unfortunately, there were a few Battles where people didn't heed that advice and there was some screaming going on, but in their defence I think it was probably just an indication of how much people wanted to succeed. Plus I suppose the adrenaline and nerves kick in too.

I think for me and Alice, it wouldn't have worked to overdo it, especially with the song we were singing. We got on really well, learning the song together and spending quite a bit of time chatting in the holding room. We often talked about her experiences on TV, which I was interested in because she had been down this route before. She was really interesting to listen to and I learned quite a bit from her.

If I am being honest, I did feel a bit of an underdog for the Battle Round. I thought that from a musical point of view, taking into account the lyrics and the melody, the song possibly suited my voice more. But I also thought from the other angle that Alice had more strengths in terms of her ability to perform and her movement on stage. She would be more confident, too, because she was pretty used to being in front of TV cameras. So overall I felt she had the edge; at the same time I thought that if I pulled out a good performance then it might just work for me.

Looking around at the other members of Team Danny made me feel even more the underdog. I thought Sean had a lot of potential because I knew that he had quite a big following on YouTube. And Karl had previously had record deals and was very experienced. I would say those were the two biggest threats to me at the time, as I perceived it. Sometimes I would sit in a room with people just listening to their credentials and I'd think, *Can I really do this? Their experience is just on a totally different level to mine!*

The problem is you will just destroy your confidence thinking like that, so in the end I just decided to focus on what I could do in terms of my own performance, and tried to block out all the professionalism and experience that the others had. My nerves were trying to get the better of me again but I have to say at this stage I was just very, very determined to make this one count. I felt that at my first blind audition I had really succumbed to my nerves and, while my performance appealed to Danny and Tom and I had received a lot of good compliments, I knew there was a hell of a lot more in the bag that I could give, if I was just able to keep a handle on my butterflies. That was my whole approach to the Battle Round. I kept telling myself: *I am going to make this performance count. If I'm going out, I want to go out doing a good performance and make my mark before I go.*

Eventually the date of the actual Battle Round came along and, as before, it was such a long, gruelling day. As a girl it is always more time-consuming to be in make-up and hair, so we had to be in the holding room early, along with the other contestants and all their coats, bags and clutter. It felt a little bit claustrophobic with everybody running up and down the corridor and doing warm-ups. Some people were sitting about playing guitars and it's easy to get caught up in all the stuff going on around you and lose your focus. For the most part I just tried to find a quiet spot and Alice was pretty much the same, so the two of us sat and did the whole 'honey and lemon' drinks thing and tried to stay away from the noise.

Our slot on stage was towards the end of the evening, and shortly before we went on we had to do a bit of filming where we walked across this bit of carpet, which effectively showed us walking into the studio. I was wearing a dress and no jacket and Alice was just wearing shorts so neither of us were particularly prepared for the snow that was coming down outside! There we were, freezing half to death in a snowstorm on this red carpet, just about to go on stage to sing for our survival in front of four mega-stars! It was all very surreal.

I figured I should go and eat something so I went to the canteen and the choice was either steak or mushroom stroganoff. I didn't fancy a big steak so I ordered the stroganoff and sat down to eat. However, I didn't realise – because I couldn't see – that they had filled this meal with loads of hot chillies and almost my first mouthful had me biting down on a whole chilli. My mouth was on fire! I grabbed some water and started trying to put out the fire in my mouth, all the time thinking, *This is not exactly the best preparation for going out to sing for your survival!*

Then we went back to the roasting hot studio again and headed to the side of the stage where there was a little waiting area. We stood next to some friends of one of the competitors and we were having a bit of banter. One of them asked me for my phone number and offered me his, and I said, 'You can give me your phone number if you like, but I can't read it!' Actually that little chit-chat really relaxed me – it was a good distraction and diffused my nerves a little bit.

I was still shaking though, partly from the cold carpet dash and partly from the butterflies. Ali came over and we did some vocal warm-ups and that really helped, too. I'd learned to do all these funny tongue movements and various singing scales and so on, but I'd also learned you have to be careful not to over-warm-up, which can be just as damaging. But mostly I was concerned about my anxiety. I actually said to Ali, 'I really hope that I keep a lid on these nerves better than I did at the audition.'

Then it was our turn to walk on stage. They introduced us both and it immediately felt very intense, because I could sense the audience were really close around us, and we were performing in this kind of boxing ring. I don't know whether they were actually closer but the atmosphere gave me the impression they were. The weird thing was that I actually felt slightly more comfortable even though it was a Battle, because there was another person on stage with me. I think at the first audition I had felt isolated because it was just me and a microphone and that was it. Whereas at least this time, even though I was battling against someone else, it still felt slightly comforting to have another person beside me on the stage. I wasn't alone.

You never actually know until you open your mouth and start to sing whether the nerves are going to overcome you. I had the very first line of 'People Help The People' to sing and once the band started and I'd sung those words I felt great. Suddenly I knew I could handle the nerves that night. I was still a little bit nervous, no doubt about it, but a lot less than at the blind audition. In fact, I was nervous in a good way because I was able to channel that energy and use it to my advantage, rather than allow myself to get carried away with anxiety. Alice did really well and had quite a powerful high note towards the end of her lines, after which I could hear the audience cheering, then we both sang the final words together. Remember, I couldn't see any facial expressions of the coaches so I didn't know whether my part had gone down well or not. In fact I couldn't see the coaches at all, just the lights.

Apparently we got four standing ovations from the coaches, which of course I couldn't see. Then it was time for their opinions. Will said it was 'beautiful, angelic, amazing' and then Jessie said she felt the song was more suited to my voice but that she believed Alice had more to give. Danny complimented Alice and said he was really proud of her then came to me and said, 'What people here don't realise is the amount of calculations that Andrea has to make before she even gets to the stage. How many steps is it up to there? Am I facing the right way? And that's even before you sang. I am really proud of you.' It wasn't broadcast but what Danny also said was that our duet had been a great joint performance, regardless of whether it was a Battle or not.

Then it came to crunch time and Danny spoke: 'I am going to go with the feeling that I always trust and that is the hairs on the back of my neck ...' When he said that I knew I had a chance because he'd said my blind audition had done that to him and if you watch it back you can see him pointing out the hairs on his arm to Will.i.am. He said this happened to him every time this person sang and then he announced who he was taking through: 'Andrea!'

I was so thrilled, I punched the air with delight and there's a clip of my mum looking overwhelmed, too.

Jessie and Danny came and helped me offstage and gave me a hug.

I was through another round of *The Voice*.

What a great night.

CHAPTER 8

SMALL INSIGHT

The very first thing that happens after a performance like that on *The Voice* is you get a camera pushed in your face! The team really want to capture your instinctive reaction and film you before you've had a chance to soak it all in, regroup and think of measured words. That way they know they are capturing a real slice of your personality. And they are right, because your adrenaline is pumping through your veins at such a speed and with all the excitement you do just genuinely say what you are thinking. There's no filter, so it's a brilliant way to showcase the contestants' real personalities to the viewing public.

Sadly, while I was chatting to the interviewer I could hear in the background that they had offered Alice up for a 'Steal' – meaning another coach could save her from elimination – but I also heard that no one did that. I felt bad, I really did, because I thought she had a lot of potential and the two of us got on so well together. I definitely wanted to see her go through. Unfortunately, that is a reality of the competition, we knew from the get-go that that's the way it happens, but when it does and it's your friend, it is brutal. I was so glad to have avoided having to stand on the stage and wait to see if someone saved me or not. I imagine it was a pretty horrible experience for her. Worse still, they then take the losing contestant off the other side of the stage and you don't really run into them.

I found Alice later in a dressing-room area and we had a bit of a chat and she wished me all the best. She was so lovely; throughout the competition she and her boyfriend came down to some of the live shows and she would text me and keep in touch. She was always so very supportive of me, which was extremely generous and classy.

It was a real shame for Alice, whereas that Battle Round experience for me was wholly positive. I felt much more confident, but we still hadn't told anyone at home yet because these were pre-recorded shows and I was still worried about jinxing myself. I certainly didn't feel that I was ahead of the pack or anything like that, don't get me wrong, especially as looking across the board there were some massive singers with big, huge ranges. Some singers had a lot of trills and riffs and all that kind of ad-libbing, but I just tried to play to my strengths. I do have a reasonably good range but vocal acrobatics are not necessarily the way I choose to sing, so I hoped that my more understated approach would perhaps make me stand out.

As I had abandoned my mushroom chilli stroganoff before the Battle Round, by the time I calmed down from the performance I was absolutely starving. So my parents, Hannah and me went to McDonald's. I remember sitting in the restaurant – should I call it a restaurant? – and we were all having a bit of a chat about what had been happening when suddenly Hannah said, 'Gosh, I think there is somebody behind us listening in and I've just seen they've got out their phone.'

Now it could have been something completely innocent but it did feel rather suspicious. Just that sudden thought made it hit home: *Actually, hold on here, this is all very public.* When you are doing pre-records you are in a bit of a bubble because it is not common knowledge among the viewing public who is left in the show (although there were sometimes leaks). But that incident in McDonald's was a sharp reminder about the whole public aspect of going on a TV show – the privacy issues, all that there.

So now we were down to the last six or seven in each team. At this stage, I can honestly say it had never crossed my mind, *not in a bazillion years*, that I might end up winning. I was just delighted to have made it through to the next round. I knew it was getting really serious now but I was still just taking it one round at a time. We had a press call in our outfits and that was my first chance to really chat with Alex, a new contestant in our team who Danny had 'stolen' from Team Jessie in the Battle Rounds. He had worked as one of the leading performers in *Thriller*, the hit Michael Jackson musical in the West End. He was very flamboyant and a really nice guy and we immediately hit it off. He was also really helpful backstage – if ever Hannah wasn't there he would happily guide me. He was great. Karl was fun too. He used to come right up to me and in a really feminine voice say, 'Hi, Andrea, this is Sarah,' and I'd just answer, 'Hello Karl, how are you?'

To be fair, most of the contestants were really helpful, especially bearing in mind that they had their own competition to concentrate on. They never left me stranded or failed to offer to help and I really appreciated that. However, for the most part, Hannah was there to do all of that so that took the pressure off them. Also I was always rather conscious that I didn't want to be seen as reliant on them to the point where I was an irritation. But I think as time went on, we got to know each other's personalities and they realised they could have a joke with me. I think that definitely alleviated the pressure and made them feel a bit more comfortable around me.

There were a couple of notable exceptions, though! I do remember one contestant in particular who seemed to struggle to understand what was going on with me. A few people weren't initially sure if Hannah was a contestant because she was backstage and around so much. Some even thought we were a duo, while a few wondered if she was on the production team. We kept trying to explain ourselves to people, that she was there to assist me, and eventually it began to sink in with most people. However this one particular contestant didn't really seem to get it and she kept coming up to me and asking really blunt questions. One day she said, 'So what can you actually see?' to which I replied, 'Well, not very much, just outlines, colours – it's all very blurry.' Then she said, 'Well, can you see this?' and she pretty much shoved her face right into mine! She was literally right up in my face; her spatial awareness was not great! I took it in good humour and most of the contestants who were standing about at the time did as well.

Fortunately that sort of reaction is not very common but it does happen. I think it was probably a good indication to me that while the vast majority of people know the etiquette around a visually impaired person and therefore understand not to do things like that, there are still a good few people out there who don't really know what is appropriate. I remember Hannah and me had quite a giggle about it afterwards, and a few of the other contestants did too. I think they were a bit surprised that she actually did it.

In the past I suppose I would have shrunk away from that situation and been a bit embarrassed but as I've got older and more comfortable with the whole sight issue, it doesn't really worry me as much. I know that it's not necessarily my problem – it's more a case of not understanding on their part rather than them being horrible or ignorant. As I've got older I've learned that the best way to deal with this sort of situation is to laugh it off and then explain it to them afterwards. It's just simple stuff, you know: 'This is what I can see, this is what I can't do, this is what I can do.' Some people will ask questions whereas other people don't feel comfortable to, so I try and explain it in the simplest terms I can, because I don't want to be boring people with the medical dictionary of Andrea Begley. Plus it is actually quite difficult for me to describe exactly what I am seeing, and to complicate matters further my sight capabilities can change. There will be certain days when I maybe recognise a colour better than other days, but it would be very marginal and it is still difficult for me to explain what I am seeing because I don't have the full visual experience in front of me, so what looks like a door to me could actually be a window.

The Voice provided its own share of challenges for my visual impairment. In your own home environment you can manage pretty well. The difficulty I always had with finding my way round at *The Voice* was that I always needed somebody with me, or I would use a mobility aid like my white stick. However, because we were changing location quite often, moving hotels very regularly and using different studios quite a lot – we went through something like four studios in the space of the time we filmed – my physical environment was almost constantly changing. And sometimes it was just very short bursts at one particular location before moving on to another a few days later. That meant I rarely had the time to learn my environment and to become comfortable to move about on my own, added to which there were always so many steps and hundreds of cables on the floor. Oh my goodness, so much stuff – cables and cases and boxes and bumps everywhere, and I mean *everywhere*. Even the amount of steps up on to the stage would change most times, so all of that combined could make it a nightmare because I was trying to orientate myself throughout a different backstage set each time.

So yes, certain things like that there can be hard to describe to people. Where I can, I try to just give people a bit of an understanding and some appreciation, because to be fair to them, if you've never come across visual impairment before then how else are you going to learn? It's hard to explain but it's important that I try. The alternatives are not so clever! I've had some friends who have tried to test themselves out by walking around their house with their eyes closed but invariably that ends in disaster!

CHAPTER 9

NOT IN A
BAZILLION YEARS

Next up was a brand new round: the Knockouts. Although the contestants were thinning out, I still wasn't getting as much time one-on-one with Danny as I would ideally have liked. That's not at all because he wasn't making the effort – oh my gosh, he was making *so* much effort – it was simply because he was so stretched trying to do all of his work for the show and look after all the contestants equally, about which he was very diligent and fair.

It was still my main ambition to spend quality time with Danny learning about songwriting and music from such an expert. He had previously made himself available to us on email, but I didn't really contemplate writing to him about songs and advice, it just felt like too much of an imposition, so for the most part I dealt directly with the music team. I felt that the song choice that the team had suggested for the Knockout was ideal for me and I was very comfortable with it. They had put forward 'Songbird' by Eva Cassidy (originally written by Christine McVie of Fleetwood Mac) and I thought that was a good song for me, so I didn't want to be unnecessarily emailing Danny when I was content with the choice anyway. It was therefore really just a case of waiting until the next rehearsal with Danny and a piano.

When we arrived for the Knockouts, there was a keyboard in one of the vocal rehearsal rooms and somebody started to play a bit of 'Superstition' by Stevie Wonder. We were all kind of jamming and singing along and I could hear quite a few of the contestants doing their little vocal tricks and whatever else, and I did think to myself again, *Cripes, this is really stiff competition here*. This was just Team Danny alone; I hadn't even really had an opportunity to hear what some of the other teams were like. At this stage you weren't really exposed to everybody else's performances, just snippets in rehearsal here and there, never full performances – and remember, it hadn't been broadcast yet so we couldn't watch them back on TV either. Then Reggie came in and he was chatting to some people and obviously I knew who it was because of his voice. He came over to me and I felt him shake my hand so as a trick I said, 'Och, how are you doing, Holly?'

We also had a press call with Danny that day and I can't even remember how the conversation started off exactly, but I think he was asking about putting us up in a hotel nearby and I said, 'No, somebody told us we were going to the Dorchester and it's on your account!' He got me back, though, because shortly after we were discussing outfits and styling for the next round and he took me to one side and said, 'Andrea, the plan for the next round is that we are going to put you in a see-through outfit but not tell you.'

Beyond that we had a very brief chat with Danny as a group. I found it quite hard to get a one-to-one chat with him because everybody was so keen to be talking to him; some of the contestants were a wee bit more confident and forthright than others, so they got talking to him more so than the likes of myself. Also, our group was quite male-dominated at this point – there was only me and Abi left out of the girls. We were the shy females while the boys all stepped forward and chatted to Danny about music and other bits and bobs.

After that we all went back to the hotel that night, late to bed, and then the next day we were straight into filming again before the Knockout. I could never have anticipated the length of the days on that show, it was incredible. Super-early starts, really late finishes and also, because you are so buzzing on the adrenaline and everything that has happened, it's not like you can go back to your hotel bed straight away and lie down and fall asleep – your body is just like, 'Go! Go! Go!' But do you know what? I loved every minute of it!

For the background filming for the Knockout stages, we had quite a few things to do. First up we went to a very fancy French restaurant where we were supposed to be interviewed chatting with Danny, but when we got there it turned out that he was ill and unable to attend, which was a real shame. So we had to do our interviews straight to camera, which I still found quite hard to be at ease with. I was improving but I was always going to be much more relaxed if they just filmed me chatting with someone.

Then we went round to the Sylvia Young Theatre School. I had never heard of it, to be honest, but it turns out that place has taught quite a few famous people in its time! Loads of people, in fact. I found it rather bizarre that it was a school – it didn't really feel like one because the students were away for holidays. I was with Hannah and she was reading all the names off the walls of the famous past students. That was really impressive.

There was a practical reason we were there, though, because part of the school was being used for the so-called 'piano routining'. This is basically where you sit around with the guys in the music team and the production team, a piano player and a vocal coach and work through the song that you are doing for the next show.

In my naivëty, I never thought of having to work out so-called 'cuts' of songs; obviously you can't get on stage and sing the full-length version because this is prime-time TV so you have a very strict allotted time. Therefore you have to create a truncated edit. If a song is cut badly, then that will affect your performance, so it was really important to make sure that you cut the song in a way that was natural and not too noticeable.

I remember very clearly at this stage that I was still feeling the pace from the previous week's efforts. It was three or four days on the trot that we'd been going to rehearsals and then the actual Battle itself, so I don't mind admitting that I was very tired. At one point, Hannah went off for a bit of a walk and some fresh air and I just waited outside a rehearsal room while everyone continued milling about, doing their thing. I was kind of chatting on and off to people but for the most part I was just sitting listening to the snatches of rehearsals and conversations and so on, just chilling out for a little bit.

When Hannah came back we were taken into a rehearsal room and they stood me next to a microphone. They wanted to get a clean version of my next song so that I could go home and practise as much as I wanted. So I sang 'Songbird' and it's funny because I would have considered my voice to be pretty tired by this point, not in the best of shape, but for some reason I could hear that I was really clicking with this performance. As you now know, I am my own worst critic but in this case I could tell it was really working.

I obviously didn't realise it at the time but I found out later that most of the people in the room were crying. Even Hannah. She always maintained afterwards – typical sister – that it wasn't actually my singing that made her cry, it was because she was looking at everybody else crying! I know 'Songbird' is a very emotional song but for some reason I really captured something that day. I don't know, maybe everyone else was just over-tired too, but the emotional side seemed to really kick in for the people watching. At the time of course I never noticed anything, I hadn't a clue, but I remember walking out at the end and Hannah came with me and told me what had happened. Other contestants came to the door to see what was going on, it was quite a scene!

It all made me feel quite good about myself in a weird way: I had done something that actually moved people to tears. Now people had been commenting on Facebook about my singing and saying it made them feel very emotional, but to hear about it first-hand was something altogether different. On the one hand, I was like, 'Oh, gosh, I don't want to make people cry!', but I also knew that my singing must have hit home to provoke that reaction. If any of the other contestants had done that I would've said that was an amazing thing to be able to move people like that. So I was weirdly happy with myself. That was a really good day.

That night we had some time off so it was our first proper chance to celebrate getting through the previous Battle Round. Hannah and me went and had a massive steak dinner in this central London restaurant which produced a rather painful bill at the end of it! That was lovely and it was just nice to be able to chill out for a couple of hours, to decompress. As much as it is fun to hang out with other contestants – and we did, we spent a lot of time with them over that period – it was also good to have that bit of time to ourselves.

The next morning I went back home and … yes, you guessed it, I went straight back to work. At this point, whenever I needed to be with *The Voice*, I was still just taking my annual leave where I could. Actually when I returned home and went to work, it was strangely therapeutic, or at least comforting, because I enjoyed the routine, the familiarity of the environment, the fact that

I knew what was going on from one minute to the next. People were not aware of the show yet so I was treated normally and that was great. A couple of colleagues started to question the amount of time off I was having, but for the most part they were just joking. It was just playful office banter – 'Oh yes, it's all right for some, swanning off on their trips here and there' – but I don't think they genuinely had any expectation that I was taking part in something like *The Voice*! So most of the time I just said I was working on something to do with my Masters. Which I was, actually … when I had a spare second.

Like I said, the Knockouts were a new round; in previous series if you got through the Battles then you automatically went into the live shows, but now the format had slightly changed so there were fewer live nights. Consequently, none of us knew very much about the Knockout Round. I couldn't fathom how it was going to work, because there were seven people in our team, an uneven number to pair off. That was pulling on my curiosity so I was very intrigued to see how they were going to arrange it. I do focus on random stuff sometimes!

The Knockout rehearsals fell at a very bad time because both Hannah and my dad were very busy with an amateur dramatics production they were doing back at home, so they weren't able to make it to the filming or indeed even to the dress rehearsals. The only person who was free to go was my mum. I kind of felt sorry for her because on the night of the filming she was like a lone ranger on her own!

On another rehearsal day, even Mum wasn't able to come over, but several members of the brilliant production team said they would come along and support and assist me. At this stage I think we had all started to gel as friends as well as work colleagues, simply because you spend so much time with these people. Actually, although I had been a little anxious when I realised I might be alone, it turned into a great day because it was my opportunity to be there on my own and to mingle like everyone else. I think sometimes people felt a little bit ... not afraid of approaching me, but because Hannah was always with me, I suppose maybe they thought there wasn't any need to talk to me. So it was really positive to see the group gel with me.

I absolutely loved my outfit for the Knockouts, this beautiful blue dress which the team stylist helped me pick. Some people had a very defined idea about what they wanted to wear to suit their image, but I didn't mind as long as the look complemented my shape really – that was what I was concerned about. I really liked the colour of this dress. I gave them the strict instructions that hot pants and a boob tube were not going to be a huge look for me. They were pretty sure that that wouldn't be the right look for 'Songbird' either, ha ha!

Joking aside, you did have to think your outfit through, because you can't sing 'Songbird' in a pair of hot pants. Well, you could but it might look totally inappropriate. You'd certainly get headlines! So I was very aware of making the right choices in wardrobe.

The rehearsals that day were actually quite scary, or should I say intimidating. Each person went up and ran through their song two or three times, while the rest of the contestants could stand and listen, so this was the very first time that we'd had the chance to hear all of the performers in full flow. At that point, if I didn't already sense the massively stiff competition, then at the end of that rehearsal I really did feel like I was up against it.

When it came to my turn to run through my song, I thought it went well and sounded good. However, the one thing I was concerned about was that maybe I wasn't all-singing and all-dancing like some of the other performers. For example, I could tell that Alex's version of 'Signed, Sealed, Delivered, I'm Yours' was amazing – obviously with his background he was a consummate performer. That did make me feel a little bit vulnerable, to be honest. So I just kept reminding myself of the tearful reaction several people had had during my piano routining of 'Songbird', and that reassured me that if I got the performance right on the night, I could make a big connection.

There was quite a good bit of fun between all of us by this point, a good craic. Karl had a bad headache from the bright lights – they were really bright, even for me and I don't see them! He was sitting with his sunglasses on and I was like, 'Yes, typical rock star, it's all gone to his head, walking about indoors with shades on already!' Then I went back up the dressing room and later Karl came in at one point and he said, 'Andrea, would it really matter if I got changed in front of you?' – thinking I would obviously not be able to see anything. I said, 'Not a bother,' but when he had finished I said, 'Karl, this is the point where I reveal that actually I can see quite a bit and in fact I just saw ALL of you getting changed!'

By this point I started to feel that whatever happened with the Knockouts, this had been a very positive experience, it had given me a fair bit of exposure, and I was really getting along with the group. You kind of don't want it to end or for people to leave because in that moment you are part of a wee family and it is very enjoyable.

People have asked me when I had my first thought of winning. Well, I can tell you that it wasn't at this point, not by a long stretch. It wasn't even on the radar then and I genuinely mean that because for me, my key thing was still to get to work with Danny one-on-one. Every round was a bonus, a total bonus. Not in a month of Sundays did I think of winning. I wasn't sure my style of singing would be enough. It might have been enough to connect with Danny and for him to take me through, but beyond that point, especially with the public vote, it was anybody's guess.

After another dress rehearsal day, it finally came to the day of the Knockouts. This was when they revealed that one person would get an automatic free pass, therefore sending them through to the live shows without having to perform. In the case of our seven, of course, this left two sets of three. It then became apparent that I would have to stand on stage with two other people while they sang their entire song, waiting for my turn to perform. That was not a particularly pleasant prospect. It was stressful and nerve-wracking enough to have to sing on my own, but the idea of having to actually stand on the stage while the other people sang their song felt very, very intense. It was just pressure, pure pressure.

I never for a second thought about me winning the free pass, because to my mind that was going to be won by Alex. I felt that as he was the 'Steal', Danny wouldn't want to risk letting him go by putting him out to sing against the others in the team.

So on the day of filming the Knockouts, I took exactly the same approach: *Here I go again, seize this opportunity to showcase myself, if this is my last performance then make it count.* It was a long day, a heck of a long day. I think we were in from before 8 a.m. until about 1 a.m. The adrenaline keeps you going – people always say that but it really does kick in. I hadn't slept particularly well the night before but to be honest I didn't sleep too good throughout the entire show. Competing in *The Voice* wasn't the best cure for any sleeping problems! When I was back at home and at work and in a routine then yes, I was fine, but when I was actually there at the show, my sleep patterns were sporadic at best. Certainly the night before a performance I wouldn't have slept great at all, no.

I spent a fair bit of time in hair and make-up, what seemed like an age. Just after I finished, I was walking around backstage when one of the crew came over to me, a guy called Tom that I really liked, and said, 'Andrea, we need you in hair and make-up now, you obviously haven't been in yet.' I'd already been in there an hour! I took it all in good jest though and I did take the mickey out of him after that.

Again nerves were still a factor at this point. I refused to let the nerves get the better of me but you just never know. As I've said, I was also strangely encouraged by the people crying at my piano routining performance, that was definitely a help. There was quite a bit of sitting about and doing nothing while you waited, which is worse than anything for nerves because it lets the pressure build up and you start to overthink things and panic and stress out. You go through so many peaks and troughs during the day.

Throughout the whole *Voice* experience, at the front of my mind I was always thinking, *Don't let yourself down, make this count*. During the Battle Round I had started to have an inkling of that little voice in my head that I told you about when I was singing live on BBC Radio Ulster: 'You don't know the words to the second verse, do you, Andrea?' and all that there. So I was always on my guard that I didn't allow myself to get nervous to the point where I couldn't concentrate on what I was doing. I knew that if the nerves got the better of me on the night, I might just take a blank.

I crammed lunch in at some point, ordering a burger with some sweet potato chips which made me feel better about myself because they weren't actual chips. Then it was time to get in the outfits for the show. When you are called to go and perform, it is only natural that the nerves spike pretty dramatically. Slightly worryingly for me, on this performance we had quite a bit of choreography. I don't mean we were being asked to dance on stage but there were lots of directions to remember both before and after the performance – where you should walk on, where you should stand, what direction you should take to leave the stage afterwards (for example if you had the free pass you went a certain way, if you didn't you went another way) and so on.

We all headed to our designated spot on stage and then Holly asked Danny who his free pass was going to be. He said it was going to be someone who had really impressed him throughout, but I wasn't really listening to every word, because I was concentrating on having to perform shortly after, that's how little I thought about the free pass being given to me. And sure enough, he did choose one of the other contestants – though it was Karl, not Alex as I had predicted. Danny went with Karl who was then taken down to what I can only describe as a little hut around the back, which is where the people who had got free passes could watch the rest of the performances.

Then Danny put myself, Abi and Alex together, so we were called forward as the first group of three while the other group of three went off. I don't mean this as any disrespect to Abi, but I still genuinely thought that Alex was going to sail through after we had performed, because he had been Danny's 'Steal'. So at this point, there was that little bit of disappointment in my mind and I found myself thinking, *Oh well, so this is the end of the line.*

On reflection, perhaps that took the edge off my nerves because I was able to sing without the expectation of going through. *This is my last performance, enjoy it, and … make it count!* Those words again. But I can't say I enjoyed that show at all. In fact it was probably one of my most horrible experiences standing on that stage, because I was last to sing … waiting … waiting … waiting to perform. We stood in a triangle with the first person to sing standing up front, and I had to wait and wait for my turn. That was really hard. You stood there listening to the crowd going wild, and the pressure and the anticipation was just immense. At least Holly didn't stop for comments from the coaches, she just kept it rolling.

Even though the songs are only a couple of minutes long, it felt a hell of a lot longer at the time. When Alex had finished, he handed me the microphone and wished me luck and then the stage manager came and positioned me out front.

I think my performance of 'Songbird' went well and I was happy with it. The song was different to the other two, which I thought was a point in my favour. And I did hear a big swell of cheers towards the end but I didn't know if that was simply because I was the last of the three to perform and they were just clapping all of us. I wouldn't say I was ecstatic but that is because I never am. However, out of the three performances I'd given so far, I felt this was my strongest, so I was content that I could walk away happy. OK, my time on *The Voice* was going to be over, but I'd done my very best.

When it came to the coaches' comments, Jessie was quite complimentary to Alex so I thought, *That's it, my days are definitely numbered*. Then she started to say something less positive, so I was going back and forth: *I must be out, no, hang on, I could still be in* ... it was this rollercoaster again. When she turned to me, she gave me the most amazing compliment, stating that every time I sang, my voice sounded like it was on a CD. To have that from Jessie was absolutely massive. It wasn't even shown on the programme but it was one of my best comments the whole way through the show.

Tom said, 'For me, the emotion came from Andrea,' then (I later found out) he pointed his finger to his heart and said, 'It hit me right there.' Will said he felt Alex was the best singer. Danny said that I never ceased to amaze him, which was wonderful to hear, but at no point was I thinking anything other than I was going home (I didn't know at this stage that I was given a standing ovation; I only found that out later).

Then it came to Danny and he went through each of the performances and said complimentary things for the most part about all of us. Then it was decision time and Danny said, 'I personally have to go with my emotions and the person that hit me in the heart most was ... Andrea.'

I was so shocked – I was through!

They took me down to see Danny and I thanked him for putting me through, telling him, 'I really did not expect that, I really didn't.' He said I had done 'an incredible job, an amazing job'.

I couldn't believe it. I was through to *The Voice* live shows.

I was in Danny's top three.

The show's top twelve.

Out of **30,000** people who'd auditioned.

I was so shocked to have beaten Alex and Abi in the Knockouts. Because of Alex's background in musicals and the fact he was such a performer on stage, compared to my very simplistic, emotional presentation, I was frankly amazed. To beat off someone with that kind of experience and background, I wouldn't say it made me think I could win, not by a long shot, but it gave me an awful big confidence boost.

After the performance I went and did an interview and my mum was there too – they filmed us meeting up and she was so emotional. She was the only one there from my family that night because the others had all got commitments they couldn't get out of and I think she felt the need to compensate for being my only supporter! It was brilliant to see her there, so exciting. Someone later told me that Mum was singing along too, so she must've enjoyed it!

Then I went back to the 'hut' backstage and, along with Karl who had already gone through, I watched the final three on Danny's team perform. I tried to watch them properly but I couldn't, I was just so far gone on the fact that I had got through; not so much that I was jumping up and down and going crazy but my head wasn't really in the right place to concentrate. At the same time you knew the cameras were on you so you were conscious of that as well. When it came to the time for Danny to make his decision about the final three, he went for Mitch. I felt disappointed for Conor and Sean but at the same time Mitch was a really nice guy, so at least I felt that the three of us would all get on reasonably well together which would be a help.

Knowing I was through to the final three in Team Danny was a phenomenal feeling. Karl, Mitch and myself got up on stage, along with Danny, of course. That's when I suddenly realised that I was the last woman standing on Team Danny. We chatted a little bit to him but a lot of it was in front of camera so it was quite formal. Then he had to rush back to do the next round of performances for the other coaches' teams.

After the show was completed, we were supposed to get more photographs done but Danny had to rush off because he had a concert overseas, I think it was, so he had to jump into a private jet straight away. I remember thinking to myself, *My goodness, I am utterly exhausted, I would not like to be running off now to do a seven-hour plane journey and play a concert on the other side of the world.* It just goes to show you, you have to be on top all the time. That was a bit of a reality check. The world of showbiz is hard graft. Danny is proof of that.

After the Knockouts, we were finished about teatime and I was quite drained at this point. I still had some interviews to do and a few other bits and pieces. Eventually I went into the canteen for some tea and buns, and I was just chatting to the people who had got through, congratulating them. Then I went upstairs to do an interview for the digital team and for some reason they were asking some really bizarre but fun questions.

'What makes you angry?'

'What is your favourite food?'

'What was the first record you ever bought?'

I won't bore you with the answers, but my favourite question was, 'What superpower would you most like?'

To which I replied, 'Perhaps X-ray vision. Well, in my case, just vision would be useful.'

CHAPTER 10

BLIND AS FOLK

In early March 2013, The Script were playing a UK tour, with three shows planned for Belfast. My sister had bought me tickets for my birthday and I had contemplated contacting Danny to say I was going to be there, and that perhaps we could meet up, but then I thought, *Och, I don't want to be annoying him.* I really didn't want to be someone who is after favours and backstage passes all the time. So in the end I didn't contact him and I went along to the Monday night's show. We had a brilliant time, and both really enjoyed the fantastic concert.

Then on the morning of the Wednesday show, I was sitting at home having my tea when my phone rang, but it was an unknown number. I let it go to voicemail and then checked the message. It was no less than Danny From The Script.

'Hi Andrea, listen, the band are playing in Belfast tonight. Do you want to come down and say hello? Give me a call back.'

Um, now there's a voicemail you never imagine getting! (And yes, I did try to save that voicemail on my phone for as long as I could! You would too!) I have to admit I laughed to myself at the absurdity of it all. So I picked up the phone pretty blooming quick and rang him back but this time I got *his* voicemail! I didn't want to leave him a message because I knew I would end up rambling and leaving a pile of rubbish, because I'm not the world's best person on voicemail. So I thought it was best to just text him and explain myself. I did that and said I had been at the show on the Monday, but didn't want to be bothering him, and that of course I'd love to meet up at the Belfast gig that night. He texted me back pretty soon after (weird moment again) and told me which hotel he was staying in and suggested that we meet up there afterwards, where it would be more private and relaxed than at the show itself.

I usually had a regular singing event that I went to on a Wednesday with a really good friend of mine, so I said to her, 'Look, I don't know if this is going to happen 100 per cent, but Danny From The Script has invited me down to his hotel after the show to meet him for a drink and a chat. I will need someone to come along with me. Do you want to join me?' That was probably one of the easiest decisions she's ever had to make!

We actually went for a wee while to our usual singing event, then I texted Danny and asked after his whereabouts and timings. He got straight back – even though he was obviously mega-busy with his gig – and gave me all the details. I'm not going to lie and say we played it cool: we totally hot-footed it over there! A couple of my other friends who were at the singing night and who knew my little secret about *The Voice* caught wind of where we were going and asked if they could tag along. I was conscious of not turning up with a big massive group of people, but at the same time I didn't want my good friends to miss out.

We all went down to the hotel and it was quite comical getting in. As I am sure is the standard when The Script stay anywhere, there was a gaggle of adoring fans standing outside, waiting to catch a glimpse of them. A big security guy was on the door and I went up with my friends and said, 'Hi, I am here to meet Danny,' and I almost laughed out loud when I said it, because I could just imagine him thinking, *Yes, of course you are, love, you and the rest of the world*. I said I could call or text Danny if that helped so I did, but I got his voicemail again, which was really embarrassing. So now I just looked like one of these crazed fans that pretends to know stars but really doesn't. So I said, 'Can you mention it to one of the guys in his team, please? That Andrea Begley is here and Danny is expecting me.'

Shortly after, one of the guys from Danny's management team came over and he was really nice and escorted us downstairs into the hotel bar, which was quite empty. I think they had closed the area off. And there was Danny sitting in one corner and he waved when he saw me. Another one of those moments.

We literally sat there and just had a good old chat for really quite a long time. As I mentioned before, I wouldn't say I was surprised that Danny was so down-to-earth and grounded, because I'd kind of anticipated that before I first met him, but the fact that he spent so long talking to me that night was great because I also knew he had to get up very early in the morning for a long journey to continue the tour. And yet he sat there and chatted away with me and my friends, not rushing us or making us feel uncomfortable in any way. We just had a real good bit of a laugh.

The best thing about it was that for once there were no cameras and no pressure and so I was able to give him a real flavour of who I was as a person and my personality. I remember an awful lot of laughs and jokes and carry on, just silly stuff. One of the things he asked me about was what genre did I think my music fitted into and I said, 'If anything I guess I'd say it was quite a folk-influenced feel.'

'Exactly,' said Danny From The Script.

'And I've already thought of the title of my debut album.'

'Really?' He seemed intrigued. 'What's that then?'

'*Blind As Folk.*'

He nearly fell off his chair; he thought this was absolutely hilarious. I think he'd always known that I was a bit of a joker but up to this point I don't think he'd realised just how irreverent I like to be. He also showed me a ring that his mum had got fixed for him (because at some point it had got broken). There was an inscription on it and he was trying to get me to feel the engraving because obviously I couldn't see it. When he handed it over to me, I said, 'Oh my goodness, Danny, I can't believe you are proposing already. It's too soon, surely?!'

It was weird for me because out of the context of the whole *Voice* experience and him being this massive public figure, it just felt like we were having a chat and a bit of fun with one of our friends. That was one thing about Danny, he always made you feel very comfortable.

He complimented me again on my voice and said it had got back to him via the team about the day when I'd made those people cry singing 'Songbird'. We spoke about the live shows and he said he'd already been having a few ideas about song choices, which was just typical of the amount of preparation and effort he put into everything. He really did care about making sure that his team came across as well as possible, which really impressed me.

Then I told him that I did a bit of songwriting.

'Great, come on, play some of your songs to me, Andrea.'

Cripes. No pressure then!

Fortunately one of my friends happened to have his guitar because we'd come from that singing event earlier. I played Danny two of my own songs, and the whole room went pin-drop quiet. I felt strangely relaxed and I think I did OK. Danny seemed to be genuinely impressed with my songs. He said it showed to him that I had an ability beyond covers and past the show itself, and that he felt there was a lot of potential. Also I think it gave him a feel for what would suit me in terms of songs for the next round of the show.

After we said goodbye and headed home, I was on a total high; it was such a buzz. To have had the chance to do that and for Danny to hear my songs … wow! I just felt that if this crazy experience never went an inch further, then I would still be happy.

That night was probably one of the most enjoyable experiences throughout the whole *Voice* experience, that opportunity to chat with Danny, then sit and play him some of my songs and have a genuine discussion with him about music, and where I wanted to go in my life. What a privilege.

After arriving back home after the Knockouts, it started to sink in that I had got through yet another round. One thought kept cropping up more than any other. *Now I have to move to London.* Up to this point I had been going back and forth between England and Northern Ireland, spending days here and there, because most of the filming had been done within pretty short spats of time. However, we were always told that the live shows would require us moving to London for a set period of time – a few weeks or whatever was required. I had never lived outside of Northern Ireland before, and that close network of family and friends at home was something that I really cherished. And, of course, it wasn't just the support – it was also the case that I knew my way around the house and my local area. Being visually impaired, it is key for me to know where I am and to be comfortable and familiar with that environment. I wouldn't say the practical challenges of being visually impaired and having to move to London concerned me overly. I knew the production team were really helpful and that I was going to be in a very safe, very well-organised environment, but it was a part of my sudden realisation that being in the live shows was going to be a whole new experience for me. For one thing, being in the last three of Team Danny felt like a massive achievement, so I still had that to absorb. Secondly, it was a live show, so that was going to be so different to the previous rounds. Finally, I also had to deal with the knowledge that I would be moving to London. So I was trying to take all that in.

I have to say, though, as much as it was very nerve-wracking, it was also *very* exciting! My attitude was very much a case of, *Whatever happens now, at least I have got this far and I can be comforted by how close I have got to the end, and even if I go out in the next round there is no shame in that, look how many people have auditioned, look at how many people went out in the Battles, look at how many people went out in the Knockouts, look at the quality of the talent.* To be standing in Danny's last three as part of the final twelve of the competition was a huge achievement. So from that point of view, I wouldn't say I was relaxed about the live shows but I was calmer than I had been before.

The other thing that lulled me into a bit of a comfort zone at this point was the fact that it was only spring and the live shows weren't going to be until June. So I felt that at least there was a period there for a couple of months to adjust to the whole idea. Also, through that period, the BBC was obviously going to air the pre-records of the show, which I was glad about because we had done so much and yet the public hadn't seen anything yet. I felt that once the shows were broadcast, it would give me a wee while to adjust and acclimatise to people recognising me, doing interviews, newspapers and all that.

In the meantime I settled back into work, studying for my uni course, plugging away at my local music projects and just doing my day-to-day normal routines. I was back at home with quite some time ahead of me in my 'normal' life before *The Voice* kicked in for the live shows.

This is perhaps an opportune moment for me to talk about some of the issues that my visual impairment creates on an everyday basis. I've already mentioned that being on the set and backstage at *The Voice*, as well as generally being away from home, presents me with a whole host of new challenges. However, that doesn't just go away because I am at home. Obviously I am much more familiar with my surroundings and to that extent life is a lot easier. That said, perhaps I can give you a little

173

perspective from 'backstage' of what visual impairment means and maybe you will come away from this with a better understanding.

First up, let me just say that it's kind of contrary to my outlook on life to talk about the impairment so directly. It is not something I think about a huge amount, it is just something I deal with as and when the need arises. That said, I have been involved with the RNIB quite a lot and this has allowed me to work on various campaigns and projects that are really aimed at educating people and increasing awareness of visual impairment. You would be surprised at how little people sometimes know about the subject.

Up until I finished uni and started my job, I had done bits and pieces with the RNIB but I couldn't devote as much time to that as I would have ideally liked, as I was studying full-time. However, I now sit on their Board of Trustees in Northern Ireland. This represents quite a change for me because although I obviously knew of the RNIB as an organisation for years, I had never really been that involved. Why? Because I suppose that I didn't want to be associated with the 'blind community' as such. This was a symptom of me having gone to a mainstream school, in that I just saw myself as a sighted person and nothing else. It wasn't until I got older and became more comfortable with my condition that I started to realise, *Hang on a minute, there are a lot of things that I can do here, in terms of campaigns and improving awareness and access.* I suppose it's the political element in me coming out to a degree. I genuinely felt this was something to which I could contribute.

Pertinently, one place where a blatant lack of understanding of the issues and challenges that visual impairment presents is at gigs. Here, access is often a major issue. Access is actually a much wider issue than getting to venues or getting around and about generally. For example, access to information itself has always been a big struggle because for the most part anything that is produced is done so for sighted people. So, for example, you go along to a gig and you are handed a programme. Well, that is pretty useless to me. Or you go to a restaurant and they hand you the menu. Ditto. Sometimes they say they have a Braille menu, which is great, of course – but I don't read Braille. I'm not alone in that.

Now there are things such as apps on your iPhone that help you read electronically, and developments such as that are great. But in terms of concerts, there are just so many issues to highlight. For example, before you even get in the venue, there are often turnstiles, which are not always do-able, they can be a bit cumbersome.

Then once you are inside there will be numerous flights of steps, varying levels of lighting, and all of this is exacerbated by the fact that there is obviously a lot of people crowded into relatively tight spaces.

Bigger venues don't necessarily guarantee that it gets any easier. In fact, I tend to shy away from vast open-air concerts because there is just too much pushing and shoving. I cannot just wrestle my way through the crowd like everybody else. Often the venue's solution is, *Let's just put everybody with a disability in a little pen at the front.* I understand their intentions, but while I don't want to be crushed or shoved about, I do want to be at the heart of the gig experience. So perhaps you can begin to see some of the problems.

On a positive note, I have noticed that in the past five years or so, it has got a lot better. Maybe that's simply down to a general improvement in the awareness of the public, helped by campaigns from the likes of the RNIB. There also seems to be a greater inclination by the venues and other public buildings to make a difference and enact change.

These are just a few of the physical obstacles and difficulties you encounter at a venue. However, what can quite often be the biggest single problem is the staff. You do come across a lot of misunderstanding from staff who don't really get that you need to be assisted. For example, just before *The Voice* live shows, I went to a gig with a friend of mine who happens to be partially sighted. First thing they did when we got in was start to gesture at us to walk a certain way to our seat, which of course neither of us could see. Often they will have a small flashlight and just point it into the darkness quite some way away. Or they might say, 'Your seat is down there.' But that is really of very little use to us; we need someone to go with us and show us exactly where the seats are.

I understand that sometimes this boils down to people looking at me and not knowing automatically that I have a disability, particularly if they see my glasses and assume I can see. Sometimes they can be pretty blunt, like, 'Are you just stupid? Can you not understand what I'm talking about?' As I have mentioned before I also don't have visual cues to follow, to try to read the situation better, so you can see how it can be quite tricky.

However, I do have to say that staff awareness has improved. You will never be able to change certain things about some venues, especially if they are older buildings which sometimes are not really very accessible at all. Due to their age, they don't have to be Disability Discrimination Act-compliant so you are not going to change the amount of steps they have. *However*, you can change people – you can explain the best way to approach someone if they need guiding; for example you should let them take *your* arm, and don't try and push them in front of you. Just very basic things like that can really make a marked improvement.

Even talking to people sometimes highlights to me how little they might understand. Often I will get asked something like, 'Can I say, "I watched that TV show last night"?' or 'Is it appropriate to say, "Did you see that dog in the street?"' Of course it is; to worry about that is just daft because at the end of the day those phrases and words are used in normal day-to-day language. Certainly, I use those words all the time, because while I don't actually see stuff physically, I still use my eyes, and it just makes more sense for me to talk like that. I wouldn't expect people to try and alter their everyday vocabulary just because they worry that they might potentially offend. They won't. Most of the blind or partially sighted people that I know would never ever want that either.

The important thing for people to remember is that it takes very little adjustment. To completely include someone who is visually impaired doesn't require you to alter your approach and attitude a huge amount. It is not the case that they need a whole load of specialist treatment and, importantly, we don't want that – I certainly don't anyway. That has been my approach for everything that I have ever done: I am doing my music on the basis of 'I am a singer', not 'I am a visually impaired singer', and I was previously an ordinary student and an ordinary worker. All visually impaired people operate on exactly the same basis as everybody else. Yes, there is the odd thing that needs changing or adapting because I physically can't do it, but if you take away anything from reading my thoughts on the subject, then let it be this: a small amount of change can make a massive difference.

CHAPTER 11

THE GENIE IS OUT OF THE BOTTLE

The first televised show on Series 2 of *The Voice* was due to air on 30 March 2013, Holy Saturday over the Easter period. However, there had been six or seven weeks of blind auditions and nobody knew which week they would be shown in. I didn't overly worry or panic because I knew that I had got through to the next round even though most people at home didn't! That said, although I had seen my audition back that day when we had met Danny for the meet-and-greet, I hadn't seen the interviews they'd done around that, or Danny's reaction in his interview after my performance, so I was looking forward (with some trepidation!) to seeing how I came across when *The Voice* was finally broadcast to the viewing public.

Then I found out I was going to be in the very first week's show! That was really exciting and I was looking forward to everybody locally *finally* knowing my big secret. The week before the broadcast I did quite a lot of interviews in the local press, because by then we could talk about the show, just not the result of my blind audition. For example, I went into BBC Radio Ulster again, this time with another DJ called Alan Simpson. My friend and guitar teacher Mark and myself went in there and did a cover of Adele's 'Make You Feel My Love', which was originally penned by Bob Dylan. The performance went really well – it was just one of those days when everything clicked. I really enjoyed it and I was delighted to hear a lot of the listeners did, too. In fact, I still get asked about that performance now, so I was really proud that I had been able to do so well. I also gave Alan a copy of my EP and said, 'Maybe you could spare a few moments to give it a listen, please?', and thankfully not only did he listen but he also played it on the radio too. Lynette Fay was also playing my EP on her show too, so I was being blessed with some brilliant radio support. In fact, people generally have been exceptionally supportive of me.

Of course, by now people at home had realised that this was where I had been disappearing off to all these months! It was such a fun week. Everybody in work was very excited and they all tried to get out of me what happened at the blind audition, but I stayed tight-lipped! I did have to tell my managers – in confidence, of course

– because I felt that they needed to know that I was going to go off to London in June, so out of courtesy to them I needed to let them know.

It also gave me the chance to say thank you to a few people who had helped me along my journey so far. For example, I went along to see Geoff, who had tipped me off on Facebook about *The Voice* being in Belfast the previous summer. He was now running a different open mic night in another bar, so I went down there to say thanks to him for that. I am sure he never thought way back then that this is where things would go. Not in a bazillion years. Me neither. But I needed to say thank you in person nonetheless. Stuff like that is important.

For the big night of my blind audition being aired on TV, we had a bit of a gathering at home. Quite a few friends and relatives came round to sit and watch it all together, which was lovely. It was really fun seeing people trying to guess if I had gone through or not; they all had their little theories! 'I think she is in Team Danny.' 'No, Team Tom, surely?' Ha ha! It was really quite hard to do the whole poker face until the programme came on, so I just kept avoiding their questions!

We all sat down and watched it together. I came on quite early in the programme, which was a relief in some ways because I think the butterflies would have got the better of me otherwise. By now I was really quite anxious to see how I was going to come across. I have to say I was very, very happy with the way they told my story and how they portrayed me, really pleased. I thought it was edited very well; I knew that they would put quite a bit of focus on me being a visually impaired person and I had kind of anticipated that because of the questions in the interview at the time. But I didn't really mind because the way I looked at it, they have to give people a snapshot of every contestant, so for example with Matt they talked about him working for the Dogs Trust. That first introduction just gives people something to connect to. In my case, they had to also point out why I needed to be guided on stage and around the corridors and things like that, because people wouldn't necessarily know why unless that was explained. So I think from that point of view it was more explanatory than anything, it wasn't focused on my visual impairment in the sense of 'This is all I am about'. They also said I had 'a unique understanding of how it feels to judge others purely on the way they sound'. I was really pleased and, all in all, I was happy with how I came across.

I was even more happy when I heard what Danny had to say in his after-show interview about my blind audition performance: 'Every part of me was electrified through it, I knew straight away from the first line of that song. That is something special, because the mood just changed in the room. That's what a megastar does, they just change it, so, wow, great moment.'

Wow indeed!

When I picked Danny as my coach on the show that broadcast night, everyone in my parents' house was so delighted. We all had a bit of a party after that, and everyone wanted to know what he was like, and all the other coaches, all that there. It was a brilliant night.

The very next day I started on interviews and press. The media were naturally intrigued by the whole 'blind girl does blind audition on the TV' story, and I understood that interest and I was fine with it. I suppose it was quite a novelty angle from the media's point of view. Then *Now* magazine contacted me and wanted to set up a photo shoot. I'd never really contemplated being asked to do such a thing so when I saw the request coming in, it was really exciting. Let me see ... would I like to spend an entire day having top stylists and hairdressers working on me, try on loads of amazing outfits, have my make-up done by some of the best make-up artists in the business? Ummm... tricky call!

It was a little bit scary in the sense that it is a popular magazine with a big readership that goes beyond the audience of *The Voice*, but then at the same time it was a great opportunity. I thoroughly enjoyed the day of the shoot; I was treated so nicely by the magazine team and the photographs looked really good, too! One thing I do remember, though, is that I will never be dismissive of professional models again – it can be pretty hard work! It was also something totally different to what I had ever done before and by this point in my life I was very open to new experiences like this. Maybe in the past I would have shied away from such things, I would have been relatively cautious. But now I really embraced it and just went for it. Fabulous day, I loved it.

I was equally delighted when *The Brendan O'Connor Show* got in touch and invited me on to their programme. That was a great experience, too. It is a huge show in Ireland and I was really excited about it because it gave me the opportunity to perform live on TV. I went on with a pal of mine on piano and another friend who played the violin, and we did my audition song, and then had an interview with Brendan. It was just a lovely day, and the whole thing was very relaxed. Obviously there was some pressure because I knew I had to perform really well, but I felt like I was there in my own right: they had

Me with Dido, Alice Barlow and Danny at rehearsals for the battle round. Very serious game face on.

Sharing a joke with Danny. It's amazing any work was done at all, we spent so much time telling stupid jokes.

Bittersweet: Even though we had become good friends, I was delighted when I was chosen ahead of Alice, because she was so talented, experienced and beautiful.

Danny's Magnificent Seven at the Knockouts.

Having sung 'Songbird' in the style of Eva Cassidy, originally by Fleetwood Mac, being congratulated by Danny for securing my place in the live shows!

Securing my place in the Final. In Final week I missed Karl and his silly jokes!

Despite the nerves and pressure of the live Final,
we all found time to goof around.

Duetting with Danny and Karl on Passenger's 'Let Her Go'.

Singing with The Script. Enough said really.

Final three … waiting for them to announce …

Hang on a minute …

Singing 'My Immortal' once more with a celebratory peck on the cheek from Danny.

With Lulu at an awards ceremony.

My debut album – *The Message*.

asked me and were obviously supportive of me, and so all I had to do was perform to the best of my abilities. That was a great day.

Once the blind audition show had finally been aired, the local community was amazing, too. There were banners in windows everywhere, people were talking about the show and championing me to do well, even the primary school at the end of my road had a big banner in the window. It was so lovely to see.

Out and about people began to stop me in the street to say hello. For example, that actual week of the first programme, I was shopping one day and three separate people stopped me to congratulate me and wish me well. People were really complimentary and talked to me very positively.

The momentum just shot up overnight. Straight away I also started to get people contacting me on Twitter and Facebook. I'd always had my own page online anyway because I was putting songs up there to promote my music, but the amount of traffic suddenly exploded. I remember looking at the amount of 'Likes' and there were literally hundreds and hundreds coming in each day. It was very exciting to be propelled into such a high profile in such a short amount of time. It was just on a whole new level, way beyond anything I could have imagined.

A few friends asked me if I was comfortable with the press interest and I can honestly say I was fine with it. I understood that was a part of the process of being on TV. Also it was massively reassuring the way that the production team from *The Voice* advised and assisted me. They never made me feel that I had to say yes to everything – it was always up to me, there was no pressure. I was quite pleasantly taken aback by the amount of interviews we were doing. *The Voice* team organised a lot of press and guided us all through the process very professionally. That was a good learning curve, because we were getting exposed to publicity in a structured way, which really helped me. But at the same time, it did start to sink in that I was definitely putting myself out there in the public eye. Naturally, as a newcomer to all of that, I also wondered what the full repercussions of that would be. Alice had spoken to me a little about this and she said you get used to that exposure, but at this stage it was all very new for me.

I think *Now* and *The Brendan O'Connor Show* were the two PR events that hit home the most, because they felt like pivotal moments. I don't consider myself to be a celebrity in any way, but that made me realise that I was now very much in the public eye. When you embark on all of this, you know that your music is what you are there to do and to focus on, but in addition the public want to know about you as a person and to try to understand who you are. Getting used to that reality has been an eye-opening experience. I definitely think there is a balance to be had between showing enough of yourself that people understand who you are, but not to the point that you lose your own privacy or identity. I sometimes can't resist being a bit mischievous, though, and on more than one occasion when people have said to me, 'Are you the girl off the telly?', I've said, 'Yes, I was on *Crimewatch* last week.'

I knew that going on *The Voice* could potentially lead to complications, but I was ready for that, it wasn't a big secret. Anyone going on to these shows can't say they never considered the media might be interested in their lives. For me, it was still definitely all about the music; I enjoyed the PR around it but the concentration was always on my songwriting and performing. That's what kept me centred and focused.

The only real concern I had with all of the press interest was not being seen as *just* a visually impaired person, because that is absolutely not all that I am. I accepted and was happy with the fact that in the early days people would inevitably be drawn to ask about that, but now I get questions about all sorts of topics and people seem to be genuinely supportive of me, rather than just seeing me as a blind girl they want to champion. Some people have actually been really blunt with me and said I only won because of the so-called 'sympathy vote', which is not a nice thing to hear obviously, but at the same time that sort of reaction was something I anticipated. It is frustrating and disappointing at times, and you can be a bit peeved off when someone points to the visual impairment as being the reason why I did well, but it didn't really annoy me as much as it might have because I expected that I would get that feedback from some quarters. I occasionally get some negativity online but that's because it's easy for people to say harsh things anonymously. I don't worry about that. Plus, I have to say, by far the vast majority of feedback has been hugely positive and complimentary.

On that point, we were given some very useful advice by the production team not to go looking for negative comments online, but just to focus on the positives and stay in touch with fans. At the end of the day, music is a subjective medium – everybody has got their view on it and whether it is in relation to my visual impairment or in relation to someone not liking my style of singing, people are entitled to their opinions. I am very comfortable with that fact, that diversity is what makes music so incredible.

If you have any ability to forsee things – which is an ironic thing for me to say! – you have to know that it is inevitable that both the media and the public will have an opinion about you.

And besides, if you think back to before the show, there I was working really hard to get my EP out, trying to get people to visit my website, to come and see me sing live, which wasn't easy. Then suddenly I've got big TV shows inviting me on, magazines running features, radio slots, newspaper interviews and loads of traffic through my website. So I need to be careful not to forget what an amazing difference this exposure has made to my profile. Last but not least, entering *The Voice* was my choice and my choice alone.

Back at home, every time the show was aired, if I was around we would have a get-together. If I was away, people still came round the house and watched everything unfold. Of course, at this point, despite all these exciting events, all my family and friends as well as work colleagues didn't know how far I had progressed in the show. I was really enjoying all the stuff I was doing but in the back of my mind I began to realise that before I knew it, I would be back in London for the live shows. Now it was about to get really serious!

CHAPTER 12

'WE CAN GIVE YOU ONE MORE DAY'

Before flying into London with Hannah for the start of the live shows, I had to go into work to finish off a project I had been pushing through. These live shows that had felt like months away were suddenly upon me, and it felt like it had been no time at all since the Knockout round. Me and Hannah moved into a beautiful, modern apartment near to the London studios where the show was filmed; we had a two-bedroom flat to ourselves, which was really lovely. However, it meant that I had to get used to a whole new layout again, which I found hard. I could manage the bedroom part and the living room but for some reason I struggled with the kitchen, I never really got used to the entire layout. Mind you, I was quite glad that we weren't going to be living in one big house together, like they do on some shows, because that would have been quite difficult for me.

It was great to have Hannah with me because I really needed her there as much as possible, just for things that everyone else takes for granted. Even simple stuff like switching on the TV for the first time or getting used to a new remote control can be tricky if you're visually impaired. I know that sounds daft, but if you can't actually see around the TV or the remote, it can be a real pain to figure things out. I usually press about forty-five buttons before I find the right one! Recently I was in a hotel where I nearly mistook the phone for a remote. Simple things that you would never really think of can actually be quite frustrating.

To further complicate the situation, I had an essay due in to my uni course the day after I arrived in London. So that very first night, I was trying to unpack, find my essentials, carefully negotiate my way around this new apartment and also finish off this essay. I'd actually emailed my tutor previously and said, 'Look, I don't think I will be able to make the deadline,' and they said, 'We can give you one more day.' This was my last module and it was truly riveting – I think the essay was called something like 'Piercing the Corporate Veil' and focused on large companies' tax strategies. You couldn't get anything more removed from music and *The Voice*, could you? But it's stuff that I find quite interesting, weirdly! Anyway, I got the essay finished and handed it all in. I think in the end I did OK with that essay, which I guess was pretty good considering how many other things were going on.

I fell asleep really late after finishing my essay and then I was up early the next morning to go straight into rehearsals for the live shows. Talk about contrast. Everybody else thought I was absolutely nuts trying to continue the Masters degree, but the way I looked at it was that I didn't want to start something and not finish it.

The week before the live quarter-final, we also did BBC *Breakfast*, where Conor, Karl, Mitch and me (with Hannah) went to Manchester late on the Wednesday night, about 11.30 I think it was, ahead of the next morning's interview. We had so much fun on the train, just sitting and chatting. It was a welcome opportunity to get away from it all. A few people recognised us but we weren't bothered too much and it was nice to just sit and chill for a couple of hours.

When we went to the TV studio the next morning, there were paparazzi standing outside. Now first thing in the morning I don't exactly look like the world's most glamorous singer! We went in and they were really nice to us so the interview went pretty well. We came straight back on the train and the plan was to rush from there into rehearsals. At Euston station the girls from *The Voice* press team met us with some sandwiches they'd bought for us, because we hadn't had any lunch and there wasn't enough time to go and get something before rehearsals. So we just jumped in this cab and started sharing these sandwiches out, only to have the taxi driver say rather curtly, 'No food in the car! No food in the car!' We couldn't believe it but he was insistent, even though our tongues were hanging out. Little did we know, but he wasn't finished yet …

In the week or so leading up to the first live show, I had been swapping song choice ideas with Danny and the team. There was a bit of routining going on, experimenting with different ideas – we were really trying to get the decision right. At one point I was supposed to be doing 'Streets Of London' but then Danny said he thought 'Ho Hey' by The Lumineers was a better choice. I was very happy with that change, as I was familiar with the new song and I liked it. Plus it was a little bit different for me, a wee bit more uptempo and it showed a different side to me as a performer.

Tuesday, Wednesday and Thursday of that week were solid rehearsal days, working with my vocal coach, working with wardrobe, just really hectic, busy days. Then at my dress rehearsal, Danny was watching and after the first rendition he came up on to the stage and said he felt I needed to move a little bit more.

Obviously this is something that I have always struggled with, so I was a little bit apprehensive. What he was saying was that because the song was more uptempo, I did need to alter my physical performance to suit. He said, 'This song doesn't require you to go crazy and jump around the stage, but maybe you could move your arms a little and be more animated that way?' Then he actually took hold of my arms and was trying to show me what he meant, which was a bit awkward and surreal. I remember laughing at myself thinking, *I am probably the envy of every female across the UK right now.* I said to him, 'I'm not going to be doing *Strictly Come Dancing* any time soon, though, Danny,' and we had a good old laugh.

Previously, we'd actually had a running joke where I'd always threaten to breakdance or finish a song off with a massive knee slide without telling him, so this was all rather funny to me, but I totally got what he was suggesting. I knew this was always the weakest part of my performance. We tried a few moves and I began to think I could do this – it wasn't such a big deal and I was really keen to make the effort. Other than that, the dress rehearsal went reasonably well and Danny seemed to be happy enough. He just kept saying to loosen up a bit more and enjoy it.

So the night of the first live show came around after a day spent in make-up, wardrobe, interviews, working with the vocal coach, all the usual stuff. At least by now I was quite familiar with the routine, I knew what to expect. Also, at this stage it started to feel a little more close-knit backstage, in the sense that because there were only twelve people left, we weren't all sprawled out across several rooms any more. There was only one holding room and so it all felt a bit more homely and comfortable.

On the other hand, though, the set for the live finals was massive and all completely new for me. We'd all had an orientation briefing for the new set to show us where everything was, where you needed to stand and so on. This was for all of the contestants, not just me. But it was just too much information to soak up all at once, so I went in again afterwards and had another look on my own with Hannah because I didn't really feel like I'd got everything into my head. Even though I know I will always have a guide, for me it is important to have a fair idea in my head of what I am actually doing. Even just getting on and off the stage can be a challenge, maybe five or six steps with no handrail or anything like that. At one point I was finding my way around with Hannah and I joked, 'This is like a torture chamber for the blind!'

One new part of this set which really was a problem was the V Room where Reggie Yates was based. Holly would always introduce the acts downstairs but Reggie was up in his little tower at the top of about forty steps, which had no rails and with the audience below on both sides. That did worry me a bit – there were just so many darn steps. It wasn't that I thought I would fall, because that could happen to anybody, not just me, but it was more just the sheer length of time it would take me to get up there. I didn't want to be taking forever to get from one part of the set to the other while they played about ten hours of holding music!

For me, not just in terms of *The Voice* but in anything I do, it's always been important to perform on a level playing field where at all possible. So I never wanted people to think, 'My goodness, the poor blind woman needs ages to get to the stage.' I was conscious of that. So it was vital that I familiarised myself with the set. By the evening I knew where the steps were, how many there were up on to the stage etc., so I did feel better. I also tried to calm myself down ... although not always successfully. *What is the worst thing that can happen to me? Er, I could fall flat on my face on live TV and become a wonderful YouTube moment for ever and a day!*

Despite the preparation and interviews, there had been quite a bit of hanging around that day. I think I ate more bags of peanuts than I ever have in my life. Then, suddenly, the performance was right upon us. They were screening the performances live then later in the evening there was a separate show for the results. For the quarter-final, there was another automatic free pass for each coach, which would leave the two remaining people to sing off against each other and go to public vote. Again I did not for a second think the free pass was going to be me.

Before the actual performances, we all had to stand on this balcony then Holly introduced 'the twelve finalists', at which point we were asked to wave at the cameras. I did exactly that but I had absolutely no idea if I was waving to the right one! I just did this giant wave and hoped for the best, knowing that I was probably just waving into oblivion.

While I was waiting for Team Danny to go on stage, I had that mountainous climb up to Reggie's V Room. Worse still, when I finally got to the top, I have never been as hot in my entire life! Obviously with the nerves and the pressure I was quite warm anyway, then when I reached the V Room it was more like Reggie's Tropical Island! A lot of the guys in the competition were wearing big jackets and they were burning up, whereas at least I only had a skirt and top on. But I felt absolutely roasted alive. When we came back down the stairs I said, 'I seriously think my face is going to melt off.'

I was guided to the side of the stage and thankfully there was a big fan keeping us all cool, which was a godsend, because the last thing I wanted to do was turn up on stage looking scalded. I chatted with my vocal coach Ali, who was always brilliant at calming my nerves. I used to appreciate what I called his 'Barack Obama speeches' and I always felt really positive afterwards! He helped to put my head in the right place and make me feel a little bit more relaxed.

One of the other elements that really helped me for the live quarter-final was that the band was situated all around me, so it felt more like a gig rather than the solo performances that I had been doing previously. I was very aware of the size of the studio audience, not that I could see them, but I had been told the capacity was something like 1800 people. A few people have asked me if, being visually impaired, playing to a large audience is different to singing in front of a small audience. I have to say my view is that it doesn't really matter: a performance is just a performance. Obviously if I know there are a thousand people watching, I might feel some more nerves but to be honest smaller gigs can be equally challenging. I knew *The*

Voice's live audience was quite large, but the more that I performed on the show the more I kind of … not *forgot* about the audience, definitely not, but I think I got more into my stride with it and the size of the crowd didn't really matter or impact on my nerves so much. However, ultimately I can't see the audience anyway, so I just have to focus on singing to the absolute best of my ability.

Suddenly my turn came. I was guided on to the stage and positioned in front of the mic. With barely a few seconds to go, Danny suddenly ran up to me on stage, gently squeezed my arm and whispered in my ear: 'Remember, relax and enjoy this, you can do it.'

The music started and right away I began enjoying myself. My nerves were under control and I was even remembering to move a little more like Danny had wanted. I wasn't doing cartwheels, don't get me wrong, but I was more animated. We had really good staging too. Danny had suggested getting a harmonica player and a violin as well so the whole set-up had a great feel about it, and I was really, really comfortable. I was very proud of the fact that I had relaxed, I'd done what Danny told me to do, and it also showed a different side of me because up until that point I had just done ballads.

I would say 'Ho Hey' was my strongest performance in the show, that and 'Songbird' probably. More so it was the most enjoyable because I didn't see what was going on but I believe that Danny and Will were getting the whole crowd going, singing and clapping along to the chant of 'Ho Hey'. It just felt like a great gig rather than a TV show. The whole atmosphere was joyous and there was a lot of warmth and good feeling in the crowd, so I thoroughly enjoyed it. That was definitely one of my biggest highlights from the show. As you know, I had been very cautious about my expectations, but I could definitely feel a momentum beginning to build.

My main time spent performing in this way was in all those dozens of competitions in Ireland, the Feis and the local shows. Now clearly that is on a whole other scale to singing in the West End five nights a week, I get that, but at the same time it was still really useful experience. The reality of performing live anywhere is that you are not always going to get a crowd to listen to you, you are not always going to hear a pin drop when you sing. It is certainly character building, as they say. I was getting into my stride and I was able to … well … not exactly switch off because there were 1800 people in the room, but I just felt more comfortable in the environment and I could sense I was getting more of a rhythm and a momentum.

People switch on to these TV singing shows and see all these contestants roll up and perform, but until you have done them yourself it's hard to imagine the compressed timeframe and the intensity of the pressure. It is really quite difficult to psych yourself up, then walk on stage, do just one truncated version of a song and then leave again two minutes later. You have to be right on the money for that brief moment. Especially knowing that your performance during those 120 seconds – that tiny sliver of time – might be perceived as the whole measure of your ability.

Well, fortunately on that quarter-final night, my 120 seconds seemed to have worked. Danny ran on the stage at the end of the song and said something like, 'You nailed it!', and the crowd seemed to be going pretty mad too. Holly then came over and said that I'd brought the house down and that everyone was on their feet! I took the opportunity to thank the audience, then Holly went to the coaches for their comments and they were all really complimentary. Danny said it was my best performance and that he was blessed to have me on his team, and Will was saying he was loving rocking the crowd with me. He was really bigging me up, telling them to 'make some noise!' Jessie said it was beautiful and Tom was emotional during my performance too, not for the first time, and that was so flattering. It was just great.

I walked off the stage feeling extremely pleased with myself and very happy that I had let myself go and enjoyed it so much. I'd got to the live shows and I'd given my best performance of the competition, so if I was to go home now, then so be it, I was totally happy with that. But I'm not going to lie, I knew that if I got through to the following week, I could duet with Danny, so, hey, I can't deny that I really, really wanted to get through!

Straight after coming offstage I went back up to the Reggie's Hot House, Super Sauna or whatever it was, and we were just chilling. I heard both Mitch and Karl's performances and was very impressed so I knew I was up against it again. What really struck me was that we embodied three very different styles of singing and songs, so I really didn't know who Danny would side with for the free pass.

We were all then sent back on stage and Danny had to do his little spiel about who he was giving the free pass to, and why. Then, to my amazement, he said he was giving the free pass to me! I was shocked but it felt like such a vindication, to have Danny voting for me like that. He said I had really stepped up my performance, which is what he had asked me to do, and I sensed that he had been testing me, to see if I could do it on the big occasion. Could I make it count?

The free pass was such a reward. I was buzzing. I vividly remember just feeling very happy and proud, not just of me but of the show itself, of the quality of the show – it was just an honour to be able to perform and be on that stage with people of that talent.

We went back up to Reggie's Super Sauna and the other contestants with free passes were in there too, similarly ecstatic. We were all getting on really well together and enjoying each other's company by this point, plus a lot of former contestants had come backstage so there was a lovely sociable atmosphere. Karl had made it through with me on Danny's team so he was obviously equally excited and proud. Conversely, the friendly atmosphere meant it also felt very sad that quite a lot of people were leaving the show that night. So there was a mixture of those who were celebrating and those who were commiserating.

Now I had to get used to the feeling that I was through to the live semi-finals. Along with Karl, I was in the last two of Team Danny.

Hold on a second, there's only eight people left … this is all getting pretty close to the finishing line here. Touching distance, in fact …

Then a thought just started to creep into the very furthest reaches of the back of my mind …

Maybe I could win this after all?

CHAPTER 13

FINALLY ... SINGING WITH DANNY

The Sunday after the live quarter-final we actually had a day off, which was sheer luxury. Hannah and me had a bit of a lie-in, then we went to a nearby town and did some shopping, which was about as strenuous a day as we could put up with. A radio presenter from back home had asked me to do an interview live on air later in the afternoon which of course I was happy to do, but I hadn't anticipated that she would phone me when I was about to try on some clothes in Next! I asked the good people in there if I could go and find an empty changing room to do the interview in and they very kindly said it was no bother. So I went in to this little cubicle and pulled the curtain across then did the interview. When we came out, the guy on changing room duty had obviously twigged who I was and he was really nice and supportive. It was really funny, though – I don't imagine too many people have done a live radio interview from a changing room in Next. Perhaps I should've chanced my arm and asked for a bit of discount? Ha ha!

Then we went home and had a relaxing evening, which was so nice after all the craziness of the past number of days. I knew the following week heading into the semi-finals would be even more intense. Apart from that very welcome day off, there was no sense of resting on your laurels – it was straight into piano rehearsals. For the semi-final week we had three songs to perform: you had your own individual song, then you had a song to do with your coach (hurray!), and we also had a group performance to do. There were only six days before the filming so it was a mountain of work to get stuck into.

There was also more PR and interviews to do, all over the place – my favourite that week was a photo shoot for *OK!* At one point during all this rushing about and hectic scheduling, we came back to Euston train station from a long, mad day of PR and once again we'd not eaten properly so we just grabbed some bags of crisps from the station platform, but as soon as we jumped in the cab, this very familiar voice barked at us, 'No food in the car! No food in the car!' Can you believe, it was exactly the same taxi driver as we'd had that time before! We took a massive fit of laughing. Ridiculous.

That was a frenetic week with rehearsals, choreography for the group performance, PR, wardrobe, make-up ... it was mad but I was loving every minute of it. This was interspersed with lots more PR – at one point Danny came out of a room to ask me to pipe down because I'd been laughing so much in an interview, but I got him back later when he was being noisy and I went in to his room and said his own words back at him. We had a good chuckle over that.

Early rehearsals were a little fraught and both Danny and I felt something about my chosen song wasn't clicking. The song we had initially picked was 'Take On Me' by A-ha. Oddly, we had rehearsed this the very next day after I got through the quarter-finals and straight away it worked; we both thought it sounded great. However, for some reason in the next few days something changed because when we came to rehearse along with the band, it just didn't sound right all of a sudden.

That said, I was conscious of trying to avoid switching songs at such late notice, because there was already enough to be learning as it was. But it just wasn't right so eventually I said, 'Danny, to be perfectly honest, I am not feeling this at all, I don't know if it's right.' He agreed and said he had the exact same feeling. Then he said, 'Come down to my dressing room, I will be hanging out there later for quite a while and we can chat about it then.'

I did have other song ideas but I didn't feel they were quite right for the semi-final. So later on I went down to Danny's dressing room and we just sat and chatted about various ideas. Danny had his guitar and he sat there strumming a few tunes to me (yes, I know what you are thinking). It was so helpful and considerate of him to give me that amount of his time. As a fan of The Script, though, it was still quite hard to give myself any perspective in that situation. On the one hand this was my current reality, but on the other hand it was never going to feel entirely normal. How could it?

One thing that has to be said is that neither Danny nor the production team ever put me under any pressure to perform a particular song. Ideas were put forward and discussed but if I wasn't comfortable then that song was binned. Unfortunately no song cropped up that we were both 100 per cent into, so we agreed to go away and think about it separately. He said, 'I'm going to head down to my studio this evening and I will give you a shout if I come up with any ideas.'

Not that long after he left I got a text and it was Danny, telling me to get down to his studio because he had found the perfect song: 'One Of Us', made most famous by Joan Osborne (most people recognise the lead lyric better than the title: 'What if God was one of us?'). Coincidentally, that had been on my list of songs that I'd had to submit way back when, at the very start of the entire *Voice* process. We had even routined the song previously but it hadn't felt right at that earlier point. But somehow Danny's suggestion to go with this track for the semi-final seemed to make perfect sense.

So Hannah and I went down to Danny's studio with a great guy called Johnny from *The Voice*'s music team. We walked into this big studio in Battersea and there were all the names of stars that had worked there before, it was a real *Who's Who* of super-celebrity musicians. Inside we found Danny working with this guy called Jim, and between them they had already worked up a two-minute edit of the song, and had actually produced some music for it so that I had a version that I could go away and learn from. I couldn't believe they'd gone to so much trouble. The quality of the recording was just amazing and the cut they had made worked beautifully. I will point out here that Danny did the same for the others on his team whenever they had been stuck – he always helped them out too. We left the studio really late after a bit of a craic; it was a great night.

Previously, Danny had mentioned that he was going to take his final two out for a day of relaxing and both Karl and I were wondering what he had planned. He just said he was taking us to a local pub. That was exciting enough for me and we were looking forward to having a bit of pure recreation time. Little did we know what Danny had really planned. It was on camera in the pub that he revealed to us the true reason he wanted to get us into central London – to take us to appear live on Radio 1's *Scott Mills Show*. I was *so* excited.

I remember getting out of the car outside Radio 1 and there were hordes of screaming fans and girls standing behind crash barriers, obviously waiting for Danny. We had never come across that before; we'd had people come to us for autographs but this was altogether different, totally manic. We went over with Danny and they all recognised us straight away, and started asking us for photos and autographs too. Danny was just the consummate professional in action, it was quite incredible to watch. He took so long shaking everybody's hands, getting photos taken and signing stuff, including various body parts! It was just second nature to him, a total masterclass. I remember thinking I needed to watch and learn from him, but at the same time I doubted there would come a time too soon when I might be mobbed outside Radio 1! He really showed us the ropes and how it could be done with class.

We eventually went inside and played Scott Mills's 'Innuendo Bingo', which mainly involved Danny getting completely soaked in water. We all had a great laugh and both Karl and I managed to stay pretty dry thankfully. What a day that was! I can always say I've been to Radio 1 on the *Scott Mills Show*, another one for the memory box.

Sometimes it was just incredible how much *The Voice* staff helped me. One day during the lead-up to the semi-final, the weather changed from being quite decent to absolutely horrendous. On one particular afternoon there was a massive, torrential downpour, and I mean torrential! Hannah said to me, 'Andrea, you are going to get completely drenched walking between the holding room and where you need to go next!' And she was right – it's not like I can suddenly break out into a sprint or anything like that! We were waiting with a few of the backstage crew, and Hannah jokingly said, 'Maybe we can get one of the security guys to give you a fireman's lift, ha ha!', and next thing I knew ... one minute I was standing on the ground and then suddenly I was being hoisted up into the air and thrown over someone's very broad shoulder as they literally ran at full speed across Pinewood Studios! I was laughing and squealing the whole way across, the poor man's eardrums must have been ringing for days! It was hilarious, great fun and really good of them to do that.

The next day we had dress rehearsals. At times every day seemed to merge into one with more rehearsals and choreography. My favourite part of that week's prep was rehearsing the Passenger song, 'Let Her Go', with Danny and Karl. I hadn't been altogether sure how this week would be structured, whether each person on the team would do their own solo with the coach or what, but when it transpired that I would be doing it with both Danny and Karl I was pleased because I thought the three of us could work together really well and we complemented each other naturally. We were all very relaxed and it felt very much like a group exercise – it didn't feel like he was the big star dictating what was going to happen, it was very equitable.

As you now know, all along I'd wanted to work more closely with Danny and I'd been lucky enough to have that time at the hotel bar as well as in the studio that evening when he worked with me on 'One Of Us'. And now I was there rehearsing with him too, which was just great. We were working out the lines, he was saying, 'You take this line, I will harmonise on that line ...' and so on, it was just such a joy. When we were working through that song, Danny said that he and the boys in the band still get nervous, that it was nothing to worry about, that energy just had to be used in a positive way. That made me feel a little bit better about the forthcoming performance; that and the fact that I loved having Danny and Karl around me on stage.

When the time came for the actual live show, I was really ready and seemed to keep a hold of my nerves quite well. I was very happy with my performance of 'One Of Us'. Fortunately this song choice was bang on the money, much more suitable for the semi-final. Afterwards the comments were great: Will said I was 'magical and enchanting' and Tom said I was 'a beautiful and angelic singer'.

I was even more excited about the song with Danny and Karl, 'Let Her Go'. That had been a song I'd potentially considered for my own solo slot so from that point of view I felt comfortable. Obviously, the main reason I was looking forward to that was because I'd be singing – *finally* – with Danny!

When it actually came to performing the song, my nerves, for once, were well under control, probably dampened down by the sheer excitement. I felt more comfortable being on the stage knowing that Danny and Karl were beside me, even if I couldn't really see them that well. For me, it felt like my first real opportunity to get *totally* into a performance, almost to forget about the competition itself and just enjoy the song for that moment. The previous performances had all been solo, so it was a very different feeling.

I think watching it back that we did a good job together. Danny is obviously a total professional and I loved singing with Karl too, who by now had become a great friend. I was happy that my voice came across OK as well. I think the three of us did indeed complement each other. It felt like a very mutually inclusive performance, it was very much a case of the three of us singing a piece *together*. I loved every minute. That performance was my best part of the night, perhaps predictably!

I was absolutely delighted to have had that opportunity to perform with Danny. It was a very surreal experience, to be a fan of his band, to sit and watch him in concert a few months' previously in Belfast, then to actually be in a position where I was standing on stage singing a song with him. It was just such a privilege. I will always look back on that as a total highlight of my time on *The Voice*. It is always there enshrined on YouTube for ever and a day (better than me falling flat on my face in my heels, eh?!). That was definitely my takeaway moment from the semi-final.

I also really enjoyed the group performance of Mumford & Sons' 'I Will Wait' because it was nice to have everybody around me on stage. We hadn't done any group performances before, so that was something different too.

Although he was my friend, Karl was also unfortunately my competition on the night. He performed brilliantly. I thought that his version of 'I Believe I Can Fly' was amazing, and in addition to his incredible vocals it worried me that that song was much better known than my choice. It was a big, epic, famous song and I thought surely that would appeal to the voting audience more? It was pure mass market. That did concern me a wee bit.

We all knew that there were no free passes for the semis, there were no other options on the table apart from public vote and I was a little bit unsure what to expect. I had never been up for public vote before. Karl had been up for public vote the week before so he knew the viewing audience had already put their faith in him once. I didn't necessarily think it was a sure bet that he would beat me, but I wasn't certain how I had been received by the audience and whether they would pick up the phone and vote for me. Up until that point, to a large extent I had been cocooned by the show, I had been protected. It had solely been down to Danny's decision, his choice and taste. However, what if that hadn't translated to the public? Maybe they might not like me as much as Danny did? I just didn't know.

Danny always used to say to us that once the show was over, we were only just starting out, the work was only just beginning, and I did worry that if the public didn't vote for me, then that path ahead could be all the more challenging.

I also, perhaps inevitably, worried that people might belittle my progress as a sympathy vote. It was never about my visual impairment, it was all about the music for me and I felt that that had come across on the show so far. But sometimes you don't know how things are going to be interpreted – or misinterpreted – by other people. So it was a whole big unknown.

After the performance show had finished airing, there was a brief gap before the results show came back on live. The time went so quickly but I do remember as I was waiting I suddenly felt really sad. If I was going home, then I was really going to miss everybody – the other contestants, the production team, the vocal coaches and, yes, Danny From The Script. You do become so much a part of that bubble, a family, that to suddenly go back to reality is a weird thought. In the past I've heard people talking about their involvement in other shows and saying it's a real family feeling which you just think is being a bit melodramatic. Yet I've felt that, too. I really didn't want to leave the comfort of *The Voice*'s world, with everything being so organised and knowing everyone around me.

I started to question what life could be like after *The Voice*. *Will I go back to my nine-to-five? Will I pursue my music more? Will people want to listen to me? Will I become a public figure or will I disappear? What happens?* Nobody knows really, and that was the same for all of us. I am sure everybody had those thoughts while we were waiting for the results, although we didn't necessarily share them.

Some people in the group had been on the wrong end of some quite negative press, and it did get to people because they are only human and sometimes that can be forgotten about in the midst of a good story. These contestants are real people who you only see a fraction of within the context of a TV show and it is very harsh to make a judgement on someone based on a few minutes of television coverage. But unfortunately that does happen. There were people that allowed that to affect them – and, worse still, affect their performances – but luckily there were others who turned it into a positive and I really admired them for that.

While I waited for the results, I tried to calm my nerves by reminding myself of some of the really positive comments I'd had from the coaches. Remember, Tom had said: 'She's just a beautiful singer, she's angelic, she's touching, she touches me right here … ' and patted his heart. As well as Will saying I was 'magical' and 'enchanting', he also said, 'It was like I was in a fairytale land.' Jessie said, 'Whatever feeling you have in your tummy right now, just hold on to that right now … that was beautiful, I just took a moment to be … how lucky we all are to be where we are in our lives. It sounded so amazing – I felt your performance, as Tom said, right in my heart.'

Danny had pointed out that I wrote my own material and played guitar then he'd said, 'It's really hard to find a song that is as good as her own stuff.' That was amazing to hear. So I used these earlier comments to try to calm my anxiety.

Then suddenly, in what seemed like a heartbeat, it was semi-final results time! There had been an escalating amount of talk in the papers about who was the favourite to win, with Leah being picked out as a clear front-runner. Ash was very popular online and Mike seemed a big contender too. We were obviously all aware of this and I personally felt very much the underdog.

I stood at the side of the set with someone from production, then I was taken to stand on stage next to

Karl, waiting for Holly to make her announcement. The wait felt like about a year. Talk about time standing still!

Then Holly said, 'The artist with the highest public vote from Team Danny and who has secured a place in next week's final is ... '

I was thinking, *It's Karl, it's Karl, it's Karl.* Before then I had thought I was in with a shot, it was at least a one in two chance, but for some reason when I walked on stage for the result, that cautious optimism vanished and I was convinced he was going through and that my time on *The Voice* was up.

Then Holly said, 'It's Andrea!'

It was just total and utter shock. Complete surprise. Karl immediately turned to me and said 'Good luck'; bless him, what a lovely guy. It was a totally amazing feeling. I said to Holly that maybe some people felt I was there because of my visual impairment and therefore to get the public vote was just a brilliant endorsement of my singing. Danny came up to me on stage and congratulated me. It was just a fantastic feeling.

I couldn't quite get my head around it.

I was in the final four.

I was a finalist on *The Voice*.

CHAPTER 14

THE FINAL WEEK

Not in a bazillion years did I think when I went to that very first audition back in the Holiday Inn in Belfast that I would end up as one of the finalists on *The Voice*. All these months later, even though I had done all that work to get where I was in the competition, it was still a big shock. Immediately following the semi-final results show, we made it back to the apartment but I only got a few hours' sleep because the next morning we had a really early start – the call time was 7:30 a.m. on the Sunday. The reason for that was Danny and I had to do piano routining first thing because he was off to the Isle of Wight Festival to play a gig with The Script. I landed rather bleary-eyed at the studio on the Sunday morning and as I was getting my make-up and hair done, I said to the girl, 'Can you make it look like I am actually alive? And not a zombie?'

I went in to see Danny and he was congratulating me on being a finalist and being really nice. One of the absolute highlights for me was that I knew I would be able to sing a duet with Danny on stage in the final, just me and him. Then he told me that we would be doing one of his own songs, 'Hall Of Fame'. I was so thrilled, what an opportunity! We worked on some other song ideas too as I'd need to be performing more than once, but apart from The Script's song nothing else felt quite right straight away, so there was more work to be done there. Each week you have to try and outdo what you did before and one of the keys to success in these shows is song choice. It is critical.

Rather cryptically, I'd been told to pack an overnight bag but I hadn't been given any details. I guessed it was something to do with Danny and a trip of some description, but I hadn't a clue what it was going to be. Then at the end of the piano routining, Danny said, 'I am sorry, Andrea, I've got to skip off early from rehearsal because I have to go and do a festival on the Isle of Wight.'

'Yes, I'd heard that, well, make sure you enjoy yourself!'

We were being filmed at this point and so the camera was on my face when he then said, 'To get us in the mood for the performance, I've arranged a little tiny outing ... Do you want to come with me to the Isle of Wight Festival?'

Ah, this is the life!

Danny said that he wanted me to be inspired to sing 'Hall Of Fame' by seeing The Script perform it in front of 60,000 people.

I'd say that should do the trick.

'Oh, and Andrea, we are going in an unconventional mode of transport.' I was thinking parachutes. It turned out to be a private helicopter.

With all of that spinning around in my mind, we headed off to catch this helicopter to the Isle of Wight. Unfortunately as passenger space was quite limited, Hannah couldn't come which was a real shame for her, so it was just me, Danny and Helen from production. We drove to this field in the middle of nowhere to find this helicopter waiting for us, but some of the glamour wore off pretty quickly when we started walking across the mud and grass which was completely covered in cow pats! I climbed inside and I could tell it was really luxurious in there, soft leather seats and all very plush. They gave me these headphones and I felt like I was in an episode of *Challenge Anneka*. I was just laughing at the whole set-up.

To be perfectly honest, I was absolutely freaking out about going up in the helicopter. People have said to me, 'How can you be worried if you can't see that you are in the sky?', but you don't necessarily have to see it to feel scared. Obviously I had vision at one time so I know what it is like to be up at a height. Plus, there is always the potential danger of these things going down, and it is quite often that you hear of helicopters crashing. Thankfully it was a calm day so I didn't really have too much to worry about and the guy who was flying us was a seasoned professional.

Danny was great, trying to put me at ease, so during the whole journey he kept describing what we were flying over – houses, fields, towns, the sea – and that did calm me down. Then he was telling all these really awful Christmas cracker-style jokes, it was a good craic. When the helicopter landed, I turned to Danny and said, 'I can't believe how smooth it was, you would hardly know you were in a helicopter,' and he said, 'Actually, Andrea, you weren't, we just pushed you in a very plush taxi and shoved it from side to side to give you the sensation that you were in a helicopter.'

We got out in another very glamorous field full of mud and cow pats to find a huge amount of press around waiting for the guys from The Script. I managed to disembark without breaking my neck, which is always a good start. We went to a hotel that had been converted into dressing rooms and I was taken straight away to The

Script's private dressing room. It's not very often that happens to you: it's a hard-knock life.

That was fabulous, obviously; I really enjoyed that. We kicked back and relaxed for a couple of hours. Danny then went and did some interviews and then we had some lunch. It was quite sunny and we were in the VIP section. I haven't really been backstage at many gigs to be honest; the nearest I've ever got to being a VIP is a Visually Impaired Person!

It was great to soak up the atmosphere for a while and I even managed to watch some of Newton Faulkner's set, which I enjoyed because I really like him. Then we went back to the dressing room and Danny officially introduced me to the band for the purposes of the TV film crew. I didn't want to be too much of a pain – not that they made me feel like that at all – but I was conscious of keeping a low profile because they had to go out and perform a full set in front of about 60,000 people. They might be The Script and they might be used to doing shows like that, but at the end of the day it was still a big performance and they have got a reputation to maintain, so I figured they had to get their heads in the right space and I didn't really want to be annoying them too much.

The guys went off and did whatever they do before a performance, getting themselves psyched up, then the next thing I know I was guided through all sorts of cable-strewn alleyways until I was standing side of stage while The Script were performing to a huge festival crowd! That was just unbelievable, fantastic. I couldn't see very much really, I could just see the movement of several figures back and forth on stage, which I assumed was Danny and the guys, and I could kind of tell there was a mass of people out there but I couldn't see any of them or what they were doing. I definitely could appreciate the huge volume of the music and also the roar of the crowd and you could hear everybody chanting the words of the songs and singing along ... I was doing the same. I was also very aware that there was a huge amount of equipment – I have never been around so many amps, speakers, cables and wires. I thought I was struggling to get round *The Voice* studios, never mind here. Thankfully I managed to get in and out of there in one piece.

I went back down after the guys had finished and settled back into their dressing room and had a brief chat with them. Then, as if all of this wasn't enough to take in, Danny said, 'Oh, and one more thing, you are going to be singing live on stage next week in *The Voice* final ... with The Script.'

This was just getting ridiculous!

I was totally gobsmacked. To be a fan and to sit and listen to their songs on your iPod and even to sing along at their shows is one thing, but I would never for a bazillion years think I would be in a position to go on stage and actually sing a song with the whole band, not just Danny.

When I was able to think straight, I said to Danny, 'You know what, I've missed a trick, I should have took the mickey out of [Danny's band members] Glen or Mark.' Danny was on this straight away and said, 'Why? What are you thinking?'

I said, 'Well, you know this whole urban myth about blind people wanting to feel people's faces, well, some people do exactly that but it's not really my thing. However, we should have done that to really wind them up.'

Danny smiled a really mischievous smile and said, 'Now, Andrea, that is a fantastic idea!'

So he called Glen over and said, 'Glen, Andrea would really like to ask you something,' and he was all very serious but I could hardly keep a straight face. I said, 'OK, Glen, sometimes, to be honest, when I meet someone for the first time, I really like to feel their face.'

Poor Glen, he is so nice, he was like, 'Sure, OK, that's no problem ...'

He stood there and I just touched his face and then put my hand up and said, 'Got you!' He was like, 'Ooh, you …' but he was really laughing and Danny was in stitches.

After that we were able to catch the end of the Bon Jovi set and then headed back to the hotel. I was sheer exhausted by the time my head hit the pillow that night, but hey, days out don't come much better than that, do they?

Back at Pinewood, the focus on song choice was getting really intense. This was the final, after all, so all three songs were critical. The plan was that you had to do a song with your coach, your 'song of the series' and a new individual song too. We had 'Hall Of Fame' with The Script already lined up and as I'd just seen them perform that on the Isle of Wight, I was really excited about that. I also pretty much knew for a while that 'Angel' was going to be my 'song of the series'. But even on the way back from the Isle of Wight, we still weren't sure about the new solo song. That was a problem; we were really struggling.

When we were heading home after the Isle of Wight, the last thing Danny said to me was, 'Right, Andrea, I am going home now and I'm going to think of this new song!' By now he was very competitive with the other coaches as well but for me, I felt I was always assured that he gave me 110 per cent.

While we were pondering song choices, the rest of the week leading up to the final was manic but totally fantastic. A couple of my cousins came over and they just had a fabulous experience: it was their first time to be in a TV studio and they were absolutely loving it. I was getting intermittent reports of my hometown of Pomeroy going completely nuts. The local pub was corralling all the support and going crazy and everybody was getting in their cars and beeping horns up and down the street – apparently it was just this mad festival atmosphere.

In London on the Monday, I had to have an appointment with this expert who was a specialist with in-ears, which are the tiny monitors that you wear inside your ear on stage so that you can hear the band and what you are singing properly. The other contestants had used them the whole way through the live shows, but I had just worked with the more old-school triangular monitor speakers that sit at the front of the stage – known as wedges – simply because none of the in-ears fitted my ears: they kept falling out. They told me I had abnormally small ears – thanks! – so the options were to either use the wedges or tape the in-ears to the side of my ears themselves. However, I didn't feel very comfortable with these things taped into my ears, essentially because my hearing is a crucial sense for me. While they were useful to help me hear the song and the music, this ad hoc set-up was cutting off all my other audible feedbacks, blocking out noises that are very useful to me. It just felt very odd and restrictive.

The RNIB will always try to dispel the myth that your hearing is improved because you can't see. The way I look at it is this: I use my hearing in a more refined way than if I wasn't visually impaired. For example, people use their eyes for visual recognition of faces. But I don't have that ability so I have to use my hearing as a voice recogniser. So whereas someone with full vision will pick up a face they recognise instantly, I have to use the tools I do have so my hearing is more tuned in because I use it more. I wouldn't necessarily say I have got super-sensitive hearing like a comic book hero or something – it's not quite like that. I just use it for different things. It can seem sensitised sometimes, like Hannah might drop something and I will point that out and yet she hasn't even noticed, but I just think that is due to me using it more than if I was not visually impaired.

However, the problem remained that Danny really felt it wouldn't work on stage with his band if I was just relying on the wedge monitors, because the volume would be too high and it would be too hard for me to follow the song. So they decided to get some in-ears made especially for me. That involved this specialist cramming very soft putty into my ears and making a mould from that: a peculiar procedure but it certainly worked!

After that I was due to see Danny at the studio and when I got there he immediately said, 'Andrea, I think I've got your new song: "My Immortal" by Evanescence.' I instantly thought that was an ideal choice. It was a song that I knew and had even sung years ago. So I was more than happy with his idea. We went down into the studio and Danny spent ages recording a version of it for me to take home and learn from, finishing quite late yet again. Relieved, I went back to the apartment feeling really good about my song choices. I later found out that that Monday was supposed to be an official day off for Danny.

An absolute highlight was when they sent all the finalists back to their families for a homecoming. That involved a really early flight to Northern Ireland – just me, Hannah and a couple of the team, plus a film crew on location who were already there ahead of us. During the journey, I had a couple of phone calls from my mum saying the town was really crazy, but I wasn't really sure what to expect when I got back home.

We landed then got a car to Pomeroy and one of the girls from the team took a few phone calls and then, as we pulled up in town, she turned to me and said, 'Andrea, look, I don't want you to be frightened here, but there are a heck of a lot of people; it is very, very crazy.' I was just thinking, *Grand, OK, I'm sure it'll be fine*. But then the car pulled up and all I could hear was this deafening noise.

For the small size that Pomeroy is, the number of people was just ridiculous. The noise was incredible, the chaos was so exciting, and I was so flattered and grateful that my hometown had come out in such numbers to support me. When I first got out of the car there was just a maul, with people touching my arms and shouting after me, asking for photographs and autographs. It was a surreal experience. I didn't feel at all frightened because I knew everybody was there to support me and they were all local people who I had grown up with – family, neighbours, friends, school mates, even school teachers – so I felt perfectly safe.

But I also remember thinking to myself, *Boy, am I glad that Danny took us to Radio 1 last week*. I'd had a little taste of what this was like and watching him in action with those girls outside the radio station had just given me some really vital tips on how to handle a situation like this.

I did a small performance and a thank-you speech then spent quite a while meeting people, chatting, signing autographs and having photos taken. I only got a few seconds with my close friends and family because there were so many people there and we were on a very tight schedule, but it was lovely to be home for a wee while.

That homecoming really illustrated to me what my parents had been saying for weeks: that my time on *The Voice* seemed to be uniting the whole community. Everybody was getting behind me. I had heard what they were saying but until I saw it for myself, I couldn't fully understand what that meant. Away from the bubble of *The Voice* in London, it was a really shocking thing to witness. We were back in London for teatime, it was that brief. It was a very tiring day, but totally amazing.

The next couple of days were also hectic. We did the *Lorraine* show, interviews with *Heat* magazine, tons of other PR, plus all our rehearsals and wardrobe, hair and make-up etc. We then did *The Radio 1 Breakfast Show* with Nick Grimshaw along with the coaches, which was really good fun. I am a big fan of Grimmy and so that was a big boost to go and meet him and do his show.

Of course, typical me, as the week went by I started to get a cold again and began to feel a little bit under the weather. I just couldn't believe it: *One of the biggest events of my life and I have to have a cold.* I did feel a tad sorry for myself, I have to say. But I just shovelled the vitamin C into me again and repeated the whole mobile pharmacy vibe with Lemsips, hot lemons, honey, everything I could think of. It wasn't a horrendous cold but it was enough to distract me. And the best way to get over a cold? Rest. No chance of that this week!

On the Wednesday we had a day of rehearsals with the band – as in The Script, not the house band, get that! – during which we had to work on 'Hall Of Fame'. To my delight Danny said, 'Andrea, I would like you to take the chorus.' *Seriously?* I was more than happy with that so I thoroughly, and I mean *thoroughly*, enjoyed the rehearsals. It was brilliant, a real pinch-yourself moment, standing there practising with The Script. Very, very pleasant.

On the Friday it was more rehearsals, more wardrobe work, the usual stuff; by now it had become, if not second nature, then a lot more a part of my routine, which I always find reassuring. By the end of that day I did feel quite beat, pretty tired. I was still feeling sorry for myself and not 100 per cent on top of the whole thing.

I started to head down one corridor towards the end of the session, excited but also a little bit glum because of my cold. Then I turned a corner and bumped into Michael Bublé, who was a guest performer for the final.

If ever you need cheering up – well, that certainly did the trick, let me tell you. Hannah happened to spot him coming out of the studio and he spoke to me for a wee while, we had a bit of a laugh together and I asked him how he was feeling about his performance. He chuckled and said, 'It's funny with these TV shows, because I go on and perform and everyone expects me to be the professional because I do this day in and day out, but if I don't do a good job then they always say the contestants are better than me!' It was a very brief few moments with him but to even have that was another lovely opportunity and an experience that I will never forget.

We didn't get out of Pinewood until really late on the Friday and by this stage I was feeling super tired. I was properly stressing out as well worrying about how the cold was going to affect my performance in the final. Ali the vocal coach told me my voice sounded fine, but to my ears it wasn't as good as I would have liked to have sounded. I was really worried that I might have come this far only to blow it at the last hurdle.

CHAPTER 15

THE VOICE FINAL

I got up on the Saturday morning of *The Voice* final and didn't feel great at all with the cold. I went over to the studio feeling somewhat disheartened because I was not on tiptop form. I was almost irritated with myself for getting ill. I started straight into the vitamin C drinks and the cold remedies – I think I must have consumed half a lemon grove and most of the honey of the country's bee population by the end of the show.

Funnily enough, my usual battle with the nerves wasn't as acute that day as I might have expected. I obviously did feel some nerves, but I mainly just felt very privileged. That final day was endlessly long but also shockingly quick, it was such a weird few hours. Some moments were slow motion, others just flew past me. We spent the whole day in the TV studio, back and forth for wardrobe, hair, make-up, interviews, rehearsals … it was very much go, go, go. I think I had half an hour to dive on one of the sofas in the holding room and grab a bit of a rest. In some ways resting too much isn't good either because you need to keep your voice warm so I was trying to strike a balance. At one point in the daytime, I said to Danny that I didn't feel 100 per cent, and he said, 'Just try and rest your voice as much as you can and try not to talk about it.'

The rest of the day went OK and once I got the first rehearsal out of the way, I felt a little more comfortable. Gradually as the day went along I relaxed and I even started to feel healthier. Weirdly enough, by the time it came round to the Saturday night final, the cold seemed to have mostly dissipated. I think maybe by that stage the lemons and the vitamin C must have been kicking in! I also think I was point-blank refusing to be ill. If ever there was a moment to make it count, this was it and I wasn't going to let some stupid head cold ruin it. Sheer determination and stubbornness on my part won the day. I just kept thinking, *No way am I going to let this stop me putting in a good performance.*

Literally just before the show, Danny said to me, 'Come over to our dressing room before you go on, Andrea, because I want to have a word with you.' So when the time came I headed over to see him. All the guys from The Script were there and Danny took my arm and said he'd made me this special drink. It contained manuka honey, lemon, ginger and all sorts of natural, fresh ingredients. 'Here, drink this, it will do you the world of good,' he said. It was one of the nicest things I have ever tasted and sure enough, it really did make me feel better.

Then he sat me down and said, 'Andrea, how are you really feeling?' I replied, 'To be honest, Danny, I am pretty nerve-wracked and I don't know whether my voice will hold out. I am a bit conscious of the fact my voice is a bit under par because I'm not feeling 100 per cent. I know I can sing and sing well enough but it is not maybe as powerful as I would like.'

He listened patiently and then said, 'Look, you are the only one that is fixating on your voice: no one else can hear a problem. Don't be worrying about getting nervous, look at what you have achieved so far, focus on the fact that you are in the final, and go out there and enjoy it. I know it is hard but just enjoy it rather than panic about the competition side of it. Stress is an indication of how much we all want to do well and be a success. But you've just got to go out there and enjoy yourself. It will be great!'

Then Glen and Mark from the band came over and said they were nervous about their performance with me too, and that made me feel even more relaxed. After that little pep talk I went back out feeling brilliant – it really helped me and Danny's special drink had also clearly had an effect. Just as well, because very shortly after speaking with The Script in their dressing room, I was called to go and do my first performance for the final of *The Voice*.

I stood at the side of the stage waiting to step up to do my first song, 'My Immortal'. I was with Ali again, and he was giving me his usual fabulous Obama speech, which kept me focused as always. Something else Danny had said to me was, 'Make sure you smile, because if you smile the crowd will too.' I went up there and started my performance; my nerves were fine and my voice seemed good, and thankfully the cold wasn't getting in the way. I did smile as Danny had advised and he was right; when I did that the crowd applauded and the atmosphere lifted another notch. Apparently they put some wings up behind me on the backdrop but obviously I couldn't see that.

The performance seemed to go down very well but there was no time to relax because I had a costume change ahead of singing 'Hall Of Fame'. Three wardrobe changes in such a short time was pretty intense for me, to be honest. So it was straight offstage, into wardrobe, get changed, then get ready to go again.

My next song was with The Script, not a sentence you often have to say. Now I thoroughly enjoyed 'Hall Of Fame', I really did. Danny came on from the back of the stage holding a torch aloft, Olympic style, while I sang the opening lines. Earlier he'd billed us as Andrea Begley's The Script! I knew from the very get-go that I would enjoy it because, while I was nervous and didn't want to make a mess of my lines, when you are on stage with the people who wrote the song and who you have followed as a fan for a long time, how can you possibly not enjoy yourself? I really let myself go for that one and it was just the best time. Danny came over halfway through and put his hand around my shoulders, which was amazing. The band did their thing too and were also very supportive of me on stage – I could feel them around me and I knew they were rooting for me. When Danny went off for a walk in the crowd, I even started ad-libbing some fills! Then Danny put his arm around me again towards the end and said, 'Come on, everybody, let's make a moment here!' It was just the best time ever.

After the performance, Holly said, 'Wow, they love you in here!', and I said what an honour it was to sing with The Script. Then Danny said, 'I loved it, tonight was Andrea Begley's The Script, it wasn't my band any more. She owned the song. We've been practising all week, I just said go out here and have some fun, and I believe one day she's gonna enter the Hall of Fame. Well done!' Then he guided me offstage to be met by my family as well as by what seemed like a pretty good round of applause.

The next part of the process involved us four finalists going back up on stage so that Holly could send one of us home and the final three would be left standing. I fully anticipated at this point that it would be me. I don't know for why – it wasn't like I hadn't given a good performance – but I expected that more likely than not it would be me going out at that point. So when Holly announced that Matt was leaving I was very surprised, to say the least.

I was down to the last three standing, along with Leah and Mike. Even I had to acknowledge that there was now the potential that I might win. Having said that, I wasn't really thinking about it that much, I was just so pleased to still be there. Also, people had been talking Leah up so much that it seemed impossible for me to win. Then I suddenly realised, *Right, I have to sing again, cripes!* So it was back off to wardrobe for another quick change and hardly any chance to prepare for what was, win or lose, my final, *final* performance on *The Voice*.

I tried to get myself into the right headspace for singing this last song. I remembered how Danny had always said to me that one of the best times he had ever heard me singing was the time when I had sat with him in that hotel bar after The Script concert. He used to say, 'That was amazing, so relaxed, if you can achieve that level of relaxation and that level of performance then you will be hard to beat.' I kept going over that thought in my mind.

My final song was my series favourite, which was 'Angel'. By then, having sung with The Script, nothing was going to ruin my night, so I went out there and gave it everything. At that stage in the game, nobody knows what is going to happen – all you can do is sell a performance as best you can sell it, because you have absolutely no control over what the public likes.

Each time I performed on that show, I felt my confidence grow a little stronger, and I was fit to let myself go a bit more and relax. The live performances where we were doing more than one song had felt more reminiscent of what I would be doing back at home – gigging. So for those shows, I was much more comfortable, because I felt I could show different strands of myself, and my performances could gradually build and build. Although in theory the pressure and expectation was ramping up with every week of the live shows that went by, the weird thing was that I actually felt more comfortable and more at ease in those live shows than on the pre-recorded weeks.

So despite this being the last song and the final, I felt I could really pull it out of the bag on the night, provided I could do what Danny had said: relax, enjoy myself, keep the nerves at bay and just let go. At the end of the day, though, you have no control over the nerves – if they hit, they hit, and that is such a scary knife-edge to be on because you don't know what your mind is going to allow you to do on the night. I just kept saying to myself, *You want to be darn sure you make this count, Andrea, no excuses. Make this count, make this count!* That was my speech to myself. Ali was with me, saying, 'You can do this, Andrea, you can,' and so by the time I came to step on stage once more, I wouldn't say I was hugely confident but I had completely zoned out of the nerves and the pressure. So I just went for it.

I actually wish I had been able to get that feeling the whole way through the show. Something just clicked. By the end of the song, I knew in myself that I had done a good job. Danny ran up to me and said that I was brilliant, and then he helped me off the stage. He said, 'That is exactly what I meant, you got it! You got back to how relaxed you were that night at the hotel in Belfast! Well done!'

Hearing that was brilliant and combined with my own feeling that it had gone well made me feel quite positive. I definitely never thought, *I've gone and won this*, but I did think, *I could be in with a shot here*.

I was escorted to the side of the stage while Leah did her performance but it was only for a few minutes as the final results were heading towards us fast. We were told previously that if you were voted as the winner, you had to sing the first song of the night again, but also be dressed in the same outfit as you had been for that performance, so it was straight back to wardrobe for a super-quick change and then back to the side of stage again. Consequently, I never really heard Leah's song but what snippets I did catch were excellent.

In what seemed like no time at all, we were standing there on stage again in a line, waiting for the announcement from Holly about who had won. I couldn't see anything, obviously – I could kind of tell there were some figures beside me, who I presumed were Mike and Leah, but I couldn't really see them at all. Then we all just held hands and I wished them both the best of luck. At this point I was still assuming that one of them would triumph. They had both been highly fancied as possible winners. Mike was very popular and I knew he had massive support while Leah was the bookies' favourite. We were all very much aware of Leah's success as she'd even had her performance of 'I Will Survive' chart at Number 8. That obviously made you think she must have a massive public following. Not that I thought that automatically meant she would win because I knew that you cannot predict these things, as we had seen the week before with Matt and Ash. But clearly she seemed to be a very strong front-runner.

Then Holly started to speak.

At this exact moment, my head was that far gone, it was all such a blur. I was trying to listen, but whatever she said at first just went over my head. She asked the coaches who they thought should win but I could barely concentrate on their responses.

Then Holly spoke again.

'The artist with the most viewer votes tonight and therefore the winner of *The Voice* 2013 is …'

It seemed to take an age standing there waiting to find out, then suddenly Holly said:

'It's Andrea!'

What?

I just squealed and put my hands up to my mouth, I was so, so shocked. I knew she'd said my name, but initially I couldn't fathom it at all. It was a whole mixture of feelings: shock, surprise, delight, fear, a mass of emotions together. *Oh my goodness, did that just happen?*

The public had picked me as their winner, incredible.

Then Danny ran up to me and shouted, 'We did it, we did it! Team Danny!'

One of the big talking points after the show was Mum's face when they announced me as the winner and about how shocked she looked. The thing is, for me, obviously I never noticed any of that. I was just focusing on the decision and what was around me.

When Holly asked me for my reaction, I just said, 'I actually can't speak, this is just … I never, ever, ever could've imagined this.' Then I thanked everyone who voted and said I would try my best to put their faith in me to good use. They then spoke to Danny who said he wanted to point out, 'How proud I am of you. It just proves that a great, great singer with a great song can knock down walls. You can smash down anything they put in front of you, you are an inspiration to me. I've learned more probably from you than you have from me. I have to say congratulations.'

I was just standing there, kind of dumbstruck, when next thing I know, the music started for my winner's song. I remember vividly thinking, *Am I actually going to be fit to sing this?* All the other contestants from the final twelve poured on the stage and they were all hugging each other and I was like, *Cripes, I actually have to sing here, this is crazy.* To make the moment even more bizarre, Holly had a slip of the tongue and said, 'Let's hear it for the voice of 2003!' instead of 2013.

The pressure was suddenly immense; I honestly didn't know whether anything would come out when I opened my mouth to sing. Fortunately I just about managed to hold it together, no more than that. I promised myself that I would never watch that winner's performance back because I knew I wouldn't be happy with it. But that was just because of the sheer shock on my part. It felt like I'd had literally milliseconds for the decision to sink in before I had to sing again.

I was never so glad to finish a song in my life! Everything was swimming around in my head – what had just happened, what that meant for me now – and I needed to take it all in. The next thing I knew, my family came up on stage (Lucy was there, as well as my Aunt Philomena and my cousin Emma too) and everybody was hugging me while all the other contestants were congratulating me simultaneously. It was manic. My heart was going hell for leather. So much to think about, so much to take in. Total overload.

You might think that seeing me so shocked was a sign that I had no faith in myself to win. That's not true, I did have faith in myself and I know that when I sing I seem to have the ability to emotionally connect with people. But I don't mind admitting I had so little thought about winning. Once I'd got to the final, obviously I knew there was a one in four chance, but because I hadn't allowed myself to think about it in any great way, when Holly announced me as the winner, it all hit me in one massive bang, this juggernaut of emotion. Maybe if I had allowed myself to contemplate the thought of winning more beforehand, it mightn't have come as such a huge shock. When it happened, it was definitely sheer surprising.

They'd even asked me in interviews, 'Do you think you can win?' And my response was always, 'I am within touching distance of it now but my achievement has been getting to this point. It isn't really something that I have focused too much energy on.' That had been my honest viewpoint.

I also think having been involved with lots of singing competitions in the past and having had a taste of being pipped to the post in a final, I knew that the best strategy was just to focus on my performance and not to worry about who was going to win.

Well, now I had to think about who had won, because it was me. It was the biggest singing competition of my life.

I had won *The Voice*.

CHAPTER 16

SUPERCARS AND SUPERSTARS

I stood on the stage with my family talking to Danny for a wee while, just soaking it all in. Then it was time to head for the holding room. My first priority, though, was getting rid of the blooming heels that I was wearing because they were killing me. They looked the part, but I was in absolute agony by the end of the night, I thought my feet were going to fall off. So I fired them off and was walking round the back of the stage barefoot, which probably wasn't really recommended in a studio like that with the floors covered in cables and equipment!

I was aiming to get back to the holding room but everybody was stopping me for photographs and congratulating me and saying hello, from other contestants to the background team and production staff – everyone seemed really happy for me. Danny had to go back to his dressing room pretty quickly, as did all the other coaches, because they had stuff to do for the show and whatnot. Quite a few of his family were there as well. As he walked off, he congratulated me again, gave me a hug and said, 'See you at the after-party!' Shortly after he did an interview in which he said, 'As much as this is an emotional moment for me, can you imagine being Andrea right now, up against everything that's gone on in her life? *The Voice* proves that dreams do come true.'

At this point backstage, someone tried to give me a piggyback because I think they were probably worried about a visually impaired girl walking around barefoot among a rats' nest of high-voltage cables! They took me to the wardrobe area so I could get changed out of my stage outfit and then finally I was guided to the holding room. Hannah was in there desperately trying to find her phone, because in the sheer hysteria of everything it had got misplaced. And there were already a lot of the other contestants in there too, so when I walked through the door they all came over to congratulate me again. That was really nice to just chat to them, and they were so excited for me, even though they hadn't won. I was really touched by how genuinely pleased they seemed to be for me.

Then one of the production team, Claire, took me to one side and said, 'Andrea, I'd like you to meet Alex Fisher, he's your new manager.' That was a really odd thing to hear. He was lovely. All the contestants had briefly met the potential winner's managers after the Knockout rounds, because the practicality of the process was such that it was too late to wait until after the final to try to set these things up. I'd already met Alex and Colin Lester, the CEO of Twenty First Artists, the management company. I'd liked them both and I remembered Colin very well because he'd had a joke about my visual impairment and really made me laugh. He obviously cottoned on right away that he could have a laugh with me. So when we met up again in the holding room that night, I knew I could get on with them well.

That said, meeting my 'new manager' literally what seemed like a few minutes after I had been announced as the winner was a very bizarre feeling. I was still pretty numb from all the events of the night so that was such a surreal moment and perhaps the very first second in which I started to think, *OK, I'm going to have my life completely changed here ... there are going to be new people, new faces, new challenges ... what is coming next?* We started to talk about the next day and what the initial plans were, and that was when it really started to hit home how different things were going to be from now on.

Before the final we had been told that whoever won the show would need to go to BBC *Breakfast* on the

Monday then do *This Morning* and Radio 2 and several other high-profile press interviews too. As I stood there chatting with Alex, all of this started to flood back into my mind. *Cripes, I'm going on* This Morning *on Monday, and Radio 2.* It all started to impact on me. I had actually got myself all organised to fly back to Belfast on Sunday morning and I was fully anticipating going into work first thing on the Monday. But it turned out that that wasn't what the audience wanted.

At this point, I wasn't at all aware that Will.i.am had stormed off the set when I was announced as the winner. Nor was I aware that he also tweeted some comments to the effect that Leah should have won and how 'perplexed' and 'sad' he was. To be honest, the last thing that I was looking at by that stage was Twitter. So I was completely oblivious at this point.

As we were all still milling around backstage, I spoke very briefly to Jessie as she was getting into her car to leave and she was really nice. She congratulated me again and then her parting words to me were to 'work hard, you have been given a great opportunity, just really go for it!' She also said not to work *too* hard, because – like Danny, Will and Tom – she knew from personal experience how demanding the music business can be.

Then I went into Danny's dressing room and spent quite a lot of time talking to him, his family and the other Script guys. He was thrilled that we had done it, delighted for me and for himself in the sense that he had beaten the other coaches. He was so proud of me first and foremost, but it was a victory for him too.

Then we headed to the after-show party, which was obviously a great, great night. I was just chattering away to everyone – contestants, production staff, the coaches who were there – and I spoke with Will at length too. I still wasn't aware of him storming off and his tweets, because in the whole hullabaloo no one had thought to mention it to me. However, Will was really kind and spoke very honestly and respectfully to me. He wished me all the best and said that if I had been his act, he would have supported me just as ferociously as he had supported Leah. I totally understood that and appreciated his honesty and it says a lot about him that he is so loyal. He also said he thought I was a very talented person and wished me all the best. He took time to talk to Mum as well, which was not something that you expect to see in your lifetime!

At some point, this guy started chatting with me and introduced himself as Conor Maynard and I was like, 'Go away, you're not really Conor Maynard,' but he was like, 'I am! Honest!' Hannah had said he was there but I thought she was taking the mickey out of me and winding me up. I just assumed it was someone pretending to be him. We had a good laugh about that.

Another fantastic moment at the party that I've already mentioned in the Foreword to this book was when my Aunt Philomena sang a duet with Tom Jones! They had both been in the music business for quite some time and after she introduced herself it seemed that they knew quite a lot of mutual connections and they were soon chatting away about all the people they had worked with down the years. Then my aunt mentioned this song she'd recorded some years ago called 'My Elusive Dream', which Tom was aware of, so they sang a few choruses of that together. That was amazing to see.

By sharp contrast, for a few moments during the after-party, when people were still all congratulating me, I suddenly felt a little bit lost. Every other week after the show had finished, you went and did an interview about your reactions and then they'd ask you how you felt now about next week. But now there was no 'next week'. At least not in terms of *The Voice*. *Am I done now?* At the party I also said farewell to the production staff and the whole team who had been like a family to me for so long. It really started to sink in that it was all over for the show and I was going to be leaving that whole comfort zone behind. I had become so comfortable and reassured by the people and the routines, so suddenly to not have that familiarity felt very odd.

Finally, after the party wrapped up and people started to head home, we collected all our stuff and, for the last time, left *The Voice* set. We went back to the apartments and I lay there, trying to get to sleep, my mind whizzing through everything that had happened, everything that had been said and done. It was just crazy.

When I woke up the next morning, the very first thing that crossed my mind was, *Did that really happen last night? Did that just take place? What the heck just happened?* Physically I felt completely drained and exhausted, but my mind was busy, trying to process everything. As I got up and started breakfast, the realisation of the night before kept hitting me in waves, over and over again ... *You won, you blooming won!*

Interspersed with these huge spikes of adrenaline when I thought about winning were spells of wondering what on earth was going to happen next. I am a pretty organised person and the one thing I have always liked to have is a definite plan of where I am going, not just literally but also in terms of my career and life in general. But what was I supposed to do now? I had to really start thinking about this on a totally different wavelength. I knew I had been given a wonderful opportunity: this was always something that I wanted, to be able to devote my time fully to music. I just felt so grateful that the audience had handed me such a great chance. Despite this slight trepidation, as I got ready for the first day of promotion I was just totally excited about what lay ahead.

That morning was full of really odd contrasts. One minute I'd be thinking about singing on stage with The Script the previous night and then I'd remember that we needed to be out of the flat in a couple of hours, so I'd be trying to sit on my suitcase and cram all my belongings into it. While I had been living in London, I'd obviously bought quite a few bits and pieces and now there was just no way it was all going to fit in, not even into this massive suitcase that I had lovingly christened the Beast. Oh, the glamour!

Understandably, that first full day of promo was ridiculously busy. I had assumed I'd be heading to the airport to fly home but instead I was now being driven to Manchester to do BBC *Breakfast*. After that, there were dozens of discussions to be had about future arrangements, and interviews to be done, both face-to-face and on the phone. It was only when I started talking to the media that I became aware of the whole Will.i.am 'storming off' incident. The journalists kept asking me how I felt knowing that Will had reacted in that way.

I am being completely honest here when I say it didn't really bother me. I think it would have bothered me more if Will hadn't spoken to me at the party and said that he was just supporting his act and that he wished me all the best. Plus he was so nice to my mum. So after chatting to him at the party, I walked away fully appreciating his view. I genuinely didn't feel any sense of bitterness or annoyance at all. The way he had spoken to me so respectfully that night completely diffused any chance of me taking offence.

Obviously I was surprised a little when the journalists told me about his reaction, because clearly there'd been no indication of that when we were chatting. But he is entitled to do and say what he wants and he was never anything other than a gentleman to me in person.

A few of the writers were pretty blunt and said that I was a surprise winner, but to be fair, it was a surprise to myself, too. It wasn't something I had anticipated at all. Another of the popular questions was about my mum and how shocked she was. That's when we found out her face was trending on Twitter – the photo of her stunned face when my name was announced was being retweeted everywhere. She became the subject of much media debate, which was hilarious for us to hear all about.

I distinctly remember one of the other questions was, 'So now that you have won *The Voice*, how do you feel about cracking America?' I was just laughing and I said, 'I think I will maybe concern myself with cracking the UK first.' Another guy said to me, 'If you make millions of pounds, what will you spend it on?' I'd honestly never even thought about money until he said that, and he went on to say some estimates were that I would make a million pounds by Christmas. Och, that all sounded ludicrous to me; that was not why I had done the show and it was not what I was thinking about having won it. I said that if I made any money I would look to be buying somewhere to live and then I joked that I might also buy myself a supercar. That's the sort of thing successful musicians buy, isn't it? Although I'm not really going to be able to drive it much!

I actually really appreciated all the press demands because it was a new routine, a new schedule and I enjoyed that very much. People were very supportive and I liked having my day so organised (I realised quickly that Alex and his management team were completely on top of their game). Alex was lovely to me and he also introduced me to Adam and Ruth who would be my tour manager and TV plugger respectively, and they were great too. I sort of laughed to myself, though: *Here I am, sitting with my 'team'*. The total unreality of it all. Yet this was my new reality.

I really enjoyed going on *Newsround*, because I had always watched that as a child. Then it was back to Radio 1 with Huw Stephens, my third time there in two weeks. He was lovely and asked me what sort of artist I aspired to be, to which I replied I really liked Laura Marling. After the interview, he said, 'Laura Marling is playing in London soon, shall I try and get you some tickets?' That was really cool of him – he had no need to do that so I was very flattered. I also went to Radio 2 and got interviewed by Patrick Kielty, fellow Northern Irelander, which was good fun.

Beyond that point, I had my first meeting with my record label, Universal, so I went and met Jo and Nick from Capitol Records there. They were very receptive to hearing my opinions, which was immediately reassuring. I hadn't prepared some big speech for when I met the label people at all, but I felt it was important to ensure that they got a sense of my identity, to try to get across who I was as an artist and what I saw in terms of my debut album. Now clearly, this wasn't something that I'd given a drastic amount of thought to, because as you know the winning of that show wasn't ever on my page, but in the two days since the final, I'd had the chance to grab five minutes to think about what I wanted to do musically. Leaving *The Voice* aside for a moment, I'd always had an ambition to do an album of my own material. I knew that the show itself was based around covers so inevitably there would have to be a fair amount of that material on my album. But I was also keen for my own songs to be heard. To meet the label so early on in the process was really reassuring and for them to be so receptive to my thoughts was brilliant. I'm looking forward to working with them in the future and I'm excited about what we can create together.

Everything seemed to be moving so quickly that week – press, TV, record-label meetings, thinking about album tracks, booking in studio time, it was insane. After I met the label, I went straight to a recording studio and did a full recording of 'My Immortal', which was released in July 2013 as my debut single. To my delight, it would reach Number 30. I was so excited that night. I listened to the Top 40, having listened to that radio show all these years as a music fan, but to tune in to hear if my song was in the chart was, I have to say, a surreal moment. When you hear your name being called out alongside all these massive stars who have had hits for Lord knows how many years, it is just very odd. I also loved the fact that the support I had enjoyed from the viewers of the show had propelled me that way. I knew I had some support out there because I had won, but in terms of the real world, outside of that *Voice* bubble, you have no idea. So for people to actually go out and buy my song and put it in the charts was a pretty phenomenal achievement.

Back in the week following my win, on the Tuesday we were invited to a party organised by *OK!* magazine at London Zoo, which was quite an unusual location. I got all my make up done and fixed up for it and then we went along and it was lovely. We met up with Leanne who had also been on the show and who I had got along with really well, plus there were a few people there from *The Voice*'s production team, so it was great to catch up with them all again. It was a lovely opportunity to relax and talk to people, take a few photos, and I think for the first time in the days since I had won I had a chance to really enjoy the moment of being the winner for a few minutes.

I did *This Morning* with Holly again and that was fun because I have watched that show for years. So finding myself on the set of *This Morning* chatting on the sofa was another pinch-me moment. Everyone there was really friendly. People had already said to me, 'Well, it must have sunk in by now,' but I can honestly say it came in fits and starts during that first week. Obviously when you are being interviewed by Holly Willoughby or Huw

Stephens or the BBC *Breakfast* team, you are fully aware that you won. There is no doubt about it, walking on to a TV show or doing an interview as the winner does give you a sense of pride in yourself and a tangible sense of achievement. It is a great crown to be able to wear. And no matter what happens, that will never be taken away from me. The audience gave that title to me, which is a great feeling to have.

Other times I'd be doing something really mundane in my hotel room and almost for a split second I'd forget myself and then suddenly it would hit me again. It's quite hard to explain but it was a very strange sensation in those moments.

Huw got me those tickets and Hannah and I went off later that week to the Laura Marling gig. It was quite funny because whenever I'm out at home, I tend to go to the same places and the staff there recognise my face and don't necessarily ask me for ID, which is a good thing because I can look very young for my age. Anyway, I was very excited to be going along to see Laura Marling but when I got to the venue, the security guy wouldn't let me in and asked me for ID! Now I had genuinely not thought to take anything with me so I was potentially stranded. I totally didn't want to say, 'Look, I've just won *The Voice*!' and all that rubbish, I knew he was just doing his job, but I was also worried about missing the gig. He asked me my date of birth and when I answered, he seemed convinced, so thankfully he let me in. I didn't feel like much of a VIP right then, though!

We saw Huw Stephens inside the gig and had a fantastic night. Again, that was a rare opportunity for me to relax and enjoy the moment. There were quite a few people coming up to me inside the venue asking for photographs and autographs and that was all very flattering, too. People were just being so nice to me the whole time. What a week that was.

After that first mad raft of press and media work was done, I flew home to Belfast, and one of the first things I did was go into work. That might sound a bit daft, given what had just happened, but there were certain things I had to organise and I was also very mindful of my contractual obligations. Plus they had been so incredibly supportive of me during my whole time on *The Voice*, there was no way I was just going to up sticks and leave them in the lurch. They'd never been anything other than 100 per cent behind me and excited for me, which was lovely, so that goodwill had to be reciprocated.

When I got to the office, I walked through the doors and there was this huge roar and a cheer went up, then a massive round of applause as they all congratulated me. Everybody wanted to come and chat. I had some photos taken, even a few with the most senior management, and everyone was ecstatic for me. They could have made my life difficult with time off and things like that, but they were always very flexible and helpful and provided I kept on top of a few things that I needed to do, they were more than happy to let me pursue my opportunity and I will always be grateful to them for that.

That evening I went out with some friends of mine from my songwriting circles, which I loved. Catching up with them was brilliant and – once again, people have just been so kind – everybody was delighted to see me and excited for me. They had all been following the show and voting for me, so I must have owed them a few drinks! It was really nice to be back in my 'normal' environment for a few hours, and stepping into my old shoes (thankfully not heels!).

The Friday was set aside to go back home to Pomeroy for a massive homecoming, and I mean *massive*! It had been organised for me by the local councillor in Cookstown and it was such a good day. I pulled up in a limo and everybody was shouting and cheering and chanting my name, it was just surreal. The real sense of community was fantastic; everybody seemed to have turned up and loads of people were wearing T-shirts and holding up banners and signs. I signed dozens of autographs and had endless photos taken. It was brilliant, such a celebratory atmosphere. I'd obviously come back previously for that very brief homecoming that *The Voice* team filmed, but this was on a whole new level. It felt a lot more palpable because I was coming back as the winner.

This was where I had grown up and these were all the people I knew – my neighbours, friends, family and work colleagues. It was very much that lovely, warm 'back at home' feeling. I did a couple of performances on the Friday night for the homecoming and I think I must have signed an autograph for everybody in the crowd. By the end of the night, my feet were sore and my wrist ached from signing things, but I didn't mind, not for one second, because all of these people had been supporting me through thick and thin. Plus on that day they had been stood waiting to see me for quite some time. It was the very least I could do.

I was aware at the homecoming that I would never be able to recreate that day again, that first time coming back home having achieved something special, so I very consciously and deliberately just sucked it all in and enjoyed it as much as I could. I was tired but the adrenaline that had been keeping me going throughout my time on *The Voice* came good again and kept pushing me forward. Underlying the tiredness of the day was an accumulative tiredness from all those weeks in the competition, then going straight into the winner's press schedule, so by the night-time I was starting to flag and feel rather tired, but I chatted and signed and took photos for as long as was required of me.

That homecoming was a lovely experience, something that I will cherish regardless of whatever happens in the future. That goes for so many things that have happened to me as a result of entering *The Voice*. I have got some fantastic memories and personal mementoes to keep and never forget.

Prior to *The Voice*, as you know, I had been working at my music and trying to make a go of things by gradually building a bigger and bigger profile. I guess for the artists who achieve success by following that path, they perhaps get used to the attention it can bring a little bit at a time. For me, I'd gone from having virtually no profile other than in and around Belfast really, to having this massive profile on a national scale. So it was a very extreme increase in attention, the profile equivalent of catching the bends, I suppose. But not for one minute did I complain, I just loved every second.

At this point, with the final having taken place only a few days previously, it still felt somehow like an extension of *The Voice*. I was still dealing with people from the show and remained very much in that mindset. As the days went by, however, it gradually began to dawn on me that that show was over and this was my new reality. I now had to make it out there as an artist, a stand-alone successful musician.

That weekend was spent at home just getting adjusted to the idea of potentially having to move to London. At least temporarily. It was a big deal for me but I immediately said that I was happy to move there if that would benefit what I was trying to do. I will do whatever is required to make this work. At least that way, I will be able to look back and feel that I put in whatever was required of me.

I only had a couple of days at home before the label needed me back near London to start work on my debut album in the studio. At this point, we weren't recording songs for inclusion on the record itself, we were just throwing ideas around and seeing what might start to sound and feel right. I was very excited about a lot of the ideas they were coming up with. Danny has also been in touch, and we have collaborated on a track called 'The Message', which is also the name of the album.

I am working with a top producer called Brian Rawling on my album. It was great being in such an amazing studio with someone like Brian. I could probably have counted on one hand the amount of days I'd previously spent in a studio. And this really was a top-notch place. I do have very strong ideas of where I want to go as an artist and a singer/songwriter, but in terms of recording, I very much consider myself to be a novice, a learner. I am totally happy saying that because I am eager to learn and keen to soak it all up.

I thoroughly enjoyed starting the album project, because not only was it very exciting, but it also felt good to be structured and organised again. After the haze and madness of the first few days following my win, over the coming weeks I started to feel a little calmer, and I was pleased to see some day-to-day routines clicking into place. For some people, that might sound terribly dull but for me I liked that idea of it being ordered and routine. I also started to find my feet in terms of what was required of me, what the people around me were trying to achieve, and to learn some of the ropes. I've quickly realised that as the winner, with a record deal and live shows coming up, my life will be just as structured now – if not more so – than when I was on *The Voice*. Everything is mapped out.

Since *The Voice* finished, I have received many messages – via emails, Facebook, Twitter or in person – saying that people have found what I have done inspiring. On the one hand it is really fulfilling to hear that you may have made a difference in someone's life, that you might have altered the way they feel and helped them to be more positive or happy about an aspect of their life that was previously more of a challenge. At the same time, it's kind of strange for me to hear, because that sort of reaction was not something I set out to create. I just entered the show because of the music. That was all it was about. In fact, I would be concerned if anyone ever thought that 'inspiring people' was remotely in the back of my mind when I started the show's auditions, because it certainly never was. I just wanted to sing to people.

I can see that people look at some of my achievements and might believe that it will help other visually impaired people think that nothing can stop them in life. That's how I look at my life: if I want to do something I will go out there and do it. However, I don't do these things to inspire people, I just do them because I want to live my life to the full. The visual impairment is just one tiny aspect of my character, so it's certainly not going to get in the way of me trying things that I want to, whether that's going white-water rafting, studying for a Masters degree or winning a big TV show. The visual impairment is irrelevant in that respect. Obviously it will throw up some practicalities but those are just hurdles that I have to get around, frustrations along the way. OK, so it might take me forever just to write a single email, or I might get annoyed because I've dropped something and I can't find it, or somebody has sent me a letter and I don't have the first clue what it says, but so what? I just get on with it – I'm used to it and it doesn't really bother me. Those frustrations can never be allowed to stop you doing what you want.

My visual impairment is not actually something that I would think or talk about very often. In fact, I rarely think that I can't see things. That is how I have adapted and got used to being visually impaired. I've only talked about it in this book because I needed to explain a little about my background and also about some of the ways that sighted people can help create change. I know some people with visual impairment don't talk about it at all, like some elephant in the room, and everybody has to have their own way of dealing with things. It would be stupid for me to say that it is all roses in the garden and everything is fine, because it's not, but I rarely think about it that way.

I would never for a second hold myself up as some amazing superhuman or whatever, not in a bazillion years. I do understand that some people have found my achievements inspiring, and many have told me that directly. So I can't deny that has happened, but it is just a huge bonus to what has gone on in my life, rather than a motivating factor.

Maybe they find what I have done inspiring because I really take the attitude of not letting my visual impairment hold me back and not really focusing on it. Perhaps people like the fact I have dipped my fingers into a lot of pies – school, A levels, university, my job, all the music stuff I've done, *The Voice* – or perhaps it's the fact that I guess I have to acknowledge that I have done pretty well at most of those things.

I can see why people might find that inspirational but I don't. As I say, I never did set out to create that reaction by entering the show. It was purely to do with the music. That said, the result is that I have had approaches from people both in terms of charities and other organisations and individuals who say they have found me inspirational and would like me to work with them to help connect with people who are challenged in a variety of ways or from difficult backgrounds, by telling them how I got over my own obstacles. Being involved in charities and talking about my achievements has been something I have been doing for the past several years anyway; it is not like I've suddenly started to do this because of the show. So I will thoroughly enjoy doing that and I look forward very much to meeting some incredible people who will, I have no doubt, inspire me.

It is nice to know that in some tiny little way overcoming the hurdles that I have might give other people some hope and perhaps some ideas about how they can live their life to the full. From a self-worth point of view, I can't deny that it is highly rewarding and pleasurable to think that I can make that kind of contribution to someone's life. Hopefully that is something I can pursue more in the coming years.

At the time of writing, I'm lined up to appear on *Songs of Praise*, *Strictly Come Dancing*, some shows aligned to the Paralympics and lots of charity gigs. Since *The Voice* finished, I have done numerous appearances and gigs, and I am also looking forward to my own shows in the autumn of 2013. In late August, I also performed at the huge Croke Park stadium in Dublin, singing the national anthem in front of 62,000 people, before an Irish hurling game. There was so much energy in the crowd, what a buzz! I've always followed my local team Tyrone since I was a kid, so to stand out on the pitch myself and sing in front of so many people was just an absolute pleasure and privilege. Performing live to people is certainly my passion and I can't wait to do those concerts and many more, because that is where I get to do the most enjoyable and important part of this whole crazy story: *the music.*

AFTERWORD

How can I avoid thinking, *What on earth is going to happen next?!* I didn't see myself coming out as the winner of *The Voice*. My involvement in the show was aimed at building up my profile, staying in as long as I could, then as I progressed through the various rounds, it was about learning as much as I could from Danny and ultimately helping me progress my music when I came back home. It didn't quite work out like that!

There isn't a manual for this, for what I have done and what I am about to do. Of course, people like Danny and all the other experts I met through *The Voice* gave me great advice along the way, but there is no book I can pick up and no masterclass I can take. I just have to get out there, work as hard as I can, and take it as far as possible.

I certainly won't fail for want of trying. My work ethic has always been strong in whatever I have done – school, A levels, uni, work, my Masters, *The Voice*. Perhaps because of my visual impairment I have had to work harder for certain things that maybe fully sighted people find easier or even take for granted. Maybe. But I do know that over the years I have enjoyed grafting really hard to succeed and I have no intention of treating this opportunity any differently. Danny called me a 'grafter' in one of his after-show interviews and I took that as a very big compliment, especially coming from him.

Of course, hard work is unfortunately not a guarantee of success. There are plenty of examples of hard-working musicians and artists who put in hundreds of hours and all the effort in the world and yet it never works out for them. I am aware of that. At the same time, I am determined to put in the work and hopefully the dividends will come on the back of that.

I also realise that no matter how concentrated and relentless my work ethic is, I can only control so much, after which I just have to hope that the public like what they hear and see and that there is a space for me in the music industry. Throughout the show, Danny constantly kept telling me this was just a start. I was always seeing him working incredibly hard on the show and with his own band, so I know what is required of me.

As for what the future holds, well, I am ready to work as hard as possible to make the most of this opportunity I have been given. While I have won a TV show and obviously gained a large appreciation out there from an audience, at the same time this is merely my starting point and I have a long way to go. There is certainly a lot of learning and work to be done, so that I can stand up in the industry and be talked about alongside other artists. I still need to make it count.

A few people have said to me, 'Wow, you have made it!' But I'm not looking at it in that way at all. Far from it. I actually just think, *I am just starting off, let's take this as far as I can.* Yes, it was a massive achievement to win *The Voice*. To have the public vote me as their winner, to succeed on that level was fantastic, but that has not made me as an artist. I have a lot more to prove and a lot more to do. It is really just my beginning. And I can't wait to get started ...

ACKNOWLEDGEMENTS

There are a huge number of people I would like to acknowledge for making this book and the story within it a reality. I owe a sincere thank you to my family, close friends, fellow musicians and songwriters from Belfast who all helped to mould and create me as a person and an artist before the *Voice* experience.

Next, I wish to thank dearly all those involved with *The Voice* from production to contestants, as well as Danny O'Donaghue, my mentor, for making the entire *Voice* experience a memorable, fun and life changing journey.

A very special thank you to Martin Roach without whom this book would not have been possible. His patience, care and ability to capture my thoughts, feelings and above all else my voice has resulted in a story I am proud of.

A word of thanks also to Julian Alexander for establishing the initial crucial links with Martin and BBC books.

My sincere thanks also goes to the publishers BBC books in particular Lizzy Gaisford, Lorna Russell and Alice Hill.

Finally, I would like to thank my team both at Capitol Records and Twenty First Artists for guiding and directing me throughout the past few months.